PREACHING

OLD TESTAMENT

PREACHING

OLD TESTAMENT

Proclamation & Narrative
in the Hebrew Bible

John C. Holbert

Abingdon Press
Nashville

PREACHING OLD TESTAMENT
Proclamation and Narrative in the Hebrew Bible

Copyright © 1991 by Abingdon Press

All rights reserved.

This book is printed on recycled, acid-free paper.

Library of Congress Cataloging-in-Publication Data

Holbert, John C.
    Preaching Old Testament : proclamation and narrative in the Hebrew Bible /
John C. Holbert.
        p. cm.
    Includes bibliographical references.
    ISBN 0-687-33870-0 (pbk. : alk. paper)
    1. Bible. O.T.—Homiletical use. 2. Preaching. I. Title.
BS1191.5.H655   1991
251—dc20   91-7712
                                                                        CIP

For Diana's courageous imagination
For Darius' creative spontaneity
For Sarah's unstinting affection

Without each of them, there would be no book
and far less of me.

CONTENTS

INTRODUCTION....................................9

CHAPTER 1 A THEOLOGICAL REFLECTION ON
NARRATIVE..17

CHAPTER 2 NARRATIVE PREACHING..........................37

CHAPTER 3 READING THE BIBLE'S NARRATIVE 55

CHAPTER 4 A PURE NARRATIVE SERMON:
THE BEST LAUGH OF ALL........................79

CHAPTER 5 A FRAME NARRATIVE SERMON:
GOD, THE MOABITE WIDOW 93

AFTERWORD 116

NOTES 118

SELECTED BIBLIOGRAPHY......................124

INTRODUCTION

There are fresh breezes blowing through the pulpits of count-less churches and synagogues. The sermon, once thought to be at death's door as an outmoded form of communication, is making a comeback. The evidence for this fact is all around us. Whenever churches are in the market for new pastoral leadership, the question that invariably appears first is "Can she preach?" An increasing number of churches print and distribute the pastor's sermon to a readership that far transcends the boundaries of the congregation who hears it. Sermon-help periodicals are sent to my office regularly. In addition to these signs, there is a marked increase of books about preaching. A rough count from my own library finds twelve books, published within the past fifteen years, which purport to be textbooks on how to preach. Many times that number of books have been published in recent years to address the complex act of preaching from various angles: communication, style, delivery, theology, history, biblical text, social context, and so forth.

One such area includes the ways in which the text of the Hebrew Bible[1] is used—or, more appropriately, not used—in the Christian pulpit. I am a trained scholar of the Hebrew Bible who attempts to teach Christian seminary students something about what it means to preach from the scriptural text. Having read the literature of the field of homiletics and listened to sermons in many churches over many years, I recognize this fact: There remains a strange silence of the Hebrew Bible in the church. One can go for more than a few Sundays in many churches without

9

ever hearing any news from the books of our scripture that pre-
cede the New Testament. That is fact, and whatever exceptions
there may be simply prove the rule.

Several scholars have addressed this question. John Bright's
1967 volume, *The Authority of the Old Testament,* discusses with great
skill the hermeneutical question of the relationships between the
testaments. Rather than answer the question of *how* one should
preach from the Hebrew Bible, Bright's book answers the question of *why* one should do so. After detailed analyses of what he
calls the "three classical solutions" to the question of the relationships between the Old and New Testaments (namely, the complete rejection of the Hebrew Bible, the use of various sorts of
typology and allegory as ways of fitting the Old to the New, and
employing a "historical, ethical Jesus" as a key with which to jetti-
son inappropriate parts of the Old), Bright asserts that the biblical reader must look to theology to find the real key to the Bible's
authority. He concludes that *"no part of the Bible is without authority,*
for all parts reflect in one way or another some facet or facets of
that structure of faith which is, and must ever remain, supremely
normative for Christian faith and practice." [2]

In his forceful arguments, Bright reminds Christian preachers
that the *entire* Bible is indeed Christian scripture, and as such
needs to be heard from the pulpit if our congregations are to
hear the full story of God's good news. Unfortunately, Bright
severely limits the ways in which that good news from the Hebrew
Bible can be understood and proclaimed. "Let us say it clearly:
The text has but one meaning, the meaning intended by its
author; and there is but one method for discovering that meaning, the grammatico-historical method." [3] Bright's statement is a
well-intentioned attempt to limit all manner of subjective readings
of the text, to provide firm grounding in the history and culture
that produced the texts. However, his statement is too simplistic
to be a helpful description of what we do when we read texts—any
kind of texts—for two reasons.

First, "the meaning intended by the author" turns out to be a
very elusive creature to discover. An enumeration of the multiple
meanings "discovered" in texts that have been subjected to serious
reading is proof of this claim. Two readings of Shakespeare's *Hamlet,*
for example, may be extremely different. In Oedipal readings,

Hamlet is motivated to his inactions because of his unresolved relationship with his mother. In Christian readings, Hamlet's inability to kill his stepfather is a result of his latent Christian unwillingness to believe in a ghost and his refusal to murder a man at prayer. Other readings add to the complexity. Which of these, if any, was the meaning intended by Shakespeare? Similarly, the book of *Jonah* has been understood in several ways. It has been interpreted to be about the universality of God, the anger of a bigoted Israelite, the dangers of false prophecy, and the dangers of narrow-minded prophets. Each of these interpretations has been vigorously and carefully defended by serious readers of *Jonah*,[4] but which was intended by the author? As this book demonstrates, careful reading of the rich narratives of the Hebrew Bible suggests that these narratives cannot be limited to "the meaning intended by the author."

The second reason that Bright's statement is simplistic is that it does not appreciate the great complexity of the act of reading. Where is the meaning of a text to be located? Is the meaning merely lodged in the text, waiting to be ferreted out by the reader, or is the reader the one who creates the meaning? The examples of Hamlet and Jonah suggest that the meaning of a text cannot be limited to the text itself; rather, the meaning is both discovered and created by the reader.

The Bible is a text that was created and preserved by a series of communities, and has been read by a community of readers. Each new reading must take those communities seriously. If this were not a true portrait of the complexity of the act of reading, how else could the book of Jonah be read successfully in so many ways? We as readers, however, are not to be thrown into complete subjectivity by the complexity of the act of reading. Thomas Long provides a helpful statement in support of this point.

> Texts have a certain reality. This is the crucial point. In a variety of ways the reality of biblical texts has signaled to the community of faith those texts' special status as scripture. Now they signal to the careful reader how they are to be read. Thus the texts themselves govern the rhetorical possibilities.[5]

Preachers may be grateful that reading is such a complex act, because the texts we are called to proclaim are almost endlessly rich in meaning. Meaning does not reside in the discovery of the perfect diamond amid the useless slag; rather, meaning resides in the very actions toward discovery. Meaning is found not only in the finished house, but also in the act of building it.

Like John Bright, other scholars have argued the theological reasons for preaching from the Hebrew Bible. In *The Old Testament and the Proclamation of the Gospel*, Elizabeth Achtemeier presents an argument that directly opposes Bright's acceptance of the authority of all scriptures. She claims, "It must be emphasized that no sermon can become the Word of God for the Christian church if it deals only with the Old Testament apart from the New." [6] She then insists that every text from the Hebrew Bible may never stand alone in the sermon but always must be paired with a text from the New Testament. Although I find this demand both hermeneutically and homiletically invalid (and I note that other scholars agree[7]), Achtemeier's work on specific kinds of texts from the Hebrew Bible points us in the right direction for ways to preach those texts.

In her book *Preaching from the Old Testament*,[8] Achtemeier offers brief but comprehensive short courses in the various types of literature in the Hebrew Bible and suggests how an appropriate recognition of these types of literature can lead to more uniquely biblical sermons. In this she follows the older work of Donald Gowan in his book *Reclaiming the Old Testament for the Christian Pulpit*. Both scholars want readers of the Hebrew Bible to take much more seriously the fact that they are reading a vast storehouse of literary forms, each of which requires specific appropriation and application in preaching. Thomas Long's *Preaching and the Literary Forms of the Bible* also shares these interests.

Because this book is concerned exclusively with the narratives of the Hebrew Bible, I am grateful for the work of Gowan, Achtemeier, and Long, each of whom provides helpful insights into this important biblical literature. However, what I find lacking or merely suggested in their work I offer here in mine.

Each of these three scholars points in a unique way to the need for this book. Gowan says, "The ancient writer used the genre which was best suited to convey the particular message which burdened him, and the question is, can that help the preacher who wants to speak to contemporaries as effectively and persuasively as

possible?" He continues, "Sometimes the text's own form of
speech can be followed; for example, something which is essentially a story may, if one is good at storytelling, be presented most
effectively by a sermon in narrative form." [9] Exactly! Gowan goes
on to urge would-be users of narrative literature to present their
interpretations "without becoming completely discursive and losing the effectiveness of the story form." [10] This book offers specific
ways in which we actually can *do* what Gowan insists we are to do.

Achtemeier also provides a reason for the need for this book.
In *The Old Testament and the Proclamation of the Gospel* she insists
that several valid methodologies must be presented to preachers
"by which the Biblical witness to God may be proclaimed and
communicated to our people;" and that such models must be presented to preachers by which the biblical witness to God may be
"related to concrete characteristics of the Biblical text." [11] Exactly!
Unfortunately, for Achtemeier—as for Gowan—these characteristics include only the broadest of genre consideration. They seldom include the details of the writing of the texts themselves.

Although Achtemeier offers a detailed rhetorical analysis of
Jeremiah 2:4-13 in her book *Preaching from the Old Testament* (an
analysis that bears some of the characteristics of the analysis I call
poetics and introduce in this book),[12] later discussions in the book
do not revert to this kind of careful examination. The result is to
oversimplify the texts she considers. For example, her reading of
the story of Joseph refuses to take the text's details with sufficient
seriousness.[13] This is ironic, given the fact that she earlier warned
us that "the first question to ask of any narrative text is, What is
going on in the story?" [14] If one really asks that question of the
story of Joseph, one will be led to a far more nuanced reading of
the story than the reading provided by Achtemeier[15]—a reading
that runs dangerously close to the most crude sort of allegory.

In this same book Achtemeier also warns preachers to avoid
something I urge preachers to try. She writes, "A preacher does
not ask such questions [i.e. the very questions that should be
asked of narratives—plot, characterization, other textual details]
in order to retell the whole biblical story in the sermon. That is
seldom necessary, and sermons that are nothing but stories are
usually not very effective."[16] This book is an argument against that
statement. Ironically, Achtemeier herself provides three very good

reasons why preachers should present, on occasion, sermons that are "nothing but stories." First and second, she says that our loss of biblical stories has brought with it a loss of the vivid and powerful language and the loss of the God portrayed so vividly and powerfully in the stories. Third, in a society of people struggling to find the story of their lives, the Bible's story is needed to provide meaning and rootedness.[17]

Thomas Long comes the closest to expressing the concerns of this book in his discussion of preaching from the Bible's narratives.[18] His discussion of the descending and ascending plot of Ruth, for example, suggests the importance of a nuanced literary reading for the task of preaching narratively. This book extends Long's discussion both theologically and literarily by offering many more examples of ways in which careful attention to the narrative as literature is crucial to the formation of a narrative sermon.

As each of these scholars indicates, there is a need for more direction in *how* to preach from the Hebrew Bible. In addition to contributing to the argument for why preaching from the Hebrew Bible is theologically important, this book offers one particularly helpful method for doing so: narrative reading and preaching. In my own experience, I have found narrative homiletics effective, satisfying, and exciting for both me and my hearers. As a means of approaching this effectiveness, satisfaction, and excitement, I invite you into the discussion in four ways.

Chapter 1 explores the question theologically. It is not enough to find a preaching style that excites and satisfies, as wonderful as that may be. We must be clear about the theological warrants that call us to preach in this way. Chapter 2 introduces narrative homiletics and discusses its definition, its problems and its possibilities. Chapter 3 introduces some of the methods and techniques of literary analysis of the narrative portions of the Hebrew Bible. These methods and techniques have most often been called *poetics*, a term that has been broadly defined as the "systematic working or study of literature as such." Finally, no book on the task of preaching is complete without some examples of what is being urged. Therefore, two of my own narrative sermons— with comments—compose chapters 4 and 5. General comments within the bodies of the sermons explain the ways in which the narrative techniques of the scriptural texts have informed the creation of my narrative sermons.

The purpose of this book is no different from that of any other preaching book: to facilitate more effective preaching and thus further spread the good news of the gospel. I write out of my own excitement for preaching that gospel. In your hands may my few suggestions find wing, and in the power of the Holy Spirit may they lift you ever upward in the calling of God in Jesus Christ our Lord.

A THEOLOGICAL REFLECTION ON NARRATIVE

"And so, Bill," I asked with anticipation in my voice, "what do you think I was talking about up there today?" I had just preached a sermon and was eating lunch with the pastor and her family after the service. Bill, his mouth full of fried chicken, began to give a quick response to my question when his father reminded him not to talk and eat at the same time. After a dutiful gulp, Bill said clearly, "I don't know." With my hopes dashed, I asked, "Well, what do you remember?" I was a glutton for punishment. A succulent chicken leg stopped in mid-flight toward Bill's waiting mouth. "That story about the old lady and her dog was sure a good one!" With that, Bill jammed the chicken leg into his mouth and gazed at me with a happy smile.

"They always remember the stories." So goes the talk among preachers as they recount their experiences of preaching to young and old; rich and poor; and black, white, red, yellow and brown. It is the stories, the anecdotes, the jokes, the biographical and autobiographical tales, the rabbinic midrashim, the newspaper snippets, and the recountings of triumphs and tragedies that people remember. In short, narratives make up the most memorable portions of the religious addresses delivered in synagogues, cathedrals, or chapels on Fridays, Saturdays, and Sundays throughout the year. Perhaps Elie Wiesel was right when he said that "God created man [and woman] because he loves stories." [1] It is also true that the humans God created in the divine image love stories as much as their creator does. Perhaps the "he" in Wiesel's words refers to both God and humans.

This book is a celebration of the love of narration that exists between God and God's creation and among the human members of that creation. In this first chapter of that celebration I discuss two theological questions that must arise first in any serious examination of the task of preaching. First, what theological warrants can one offer for preaching narratively? It is not enough to say that because everyone seems to like stories, we preachers should become better storytellers and should tell vivid biblical narratives for our sermons. That may be one important reason for pursuing narratives as sermons, but it is hardly the definitive reason. Humankind's love of stories does lead us, however, to a second question that has important theological implications: Is there a so-called narrative quality of experience? If so, what does that definition of experience have to say about the possibility of a narrative homiletics?

Even at this introductory stage of the discussion, a careful reader can see that these two questions are not completely independent of one another. Wiesel's claim that God's love of stories is the very reason for human creation and my additional claim that humans love stories as a result of their creation by a story-loving creator suggest that our perception of God as a storyteller and story-lover has a profound effect on the way we perceive our experience of and in a world created and sustained by such a God. Thus, the reader should be warned that although the two questions will be addressed separately in this chapter, it will be impossible to separate them completely.

Theology and Narrative

When properly read and appropriated, the biblical narrative tells us *how* to preach as surely as it tells us *what* to preach. The biblical narrative presents "God's word in the world" and helps us "to align one's *mode* and *matter* of preaching accordingly" (emphasis mine).[2]

The primary warrant for pursuing a narrative homiletics arises from the primary source for all Jewish and Christian theology: The Bible. Regardless of how differently the Bible is evaluated by these two faith communities, all theological reflection pursued in these two communities either begins in or refers significantly to the Bible.

> Scripture is the primary source and criterion for Christian doctrine. . . . The Bible bears authentic testimony to God's self-disclosure in the life, death, and resurrection of Jesus Christ as well as in God's work of creation, in the pilgrimage of Israel, and in the Holy Spirit's ongoing activity in human history.[3]

By referring to the Bible as a "source" for Christian doctrine, this statement assumes that doctrine both originates and results from the Bible. In the scriptures we find not only our inspiration for theological reflection but also the very reasons why such reflection is necessary. The Bible compels us to interpret its words for each new generation, and in that interpretation we find the substance of our doctrine and the content of our theological reflection. Furthermore, by naming the Bible a "criterion," this statement affirms that the Bible supplies a standard, a rule, or a test by which theological judgments may be evaluated. Therefore, "the Bible serves both as a source of our faith and as the basic criterion by which the truth and fidelity of any interpretation of faith is measured."[4]

If we stopped here in our announcement of the primacy of scripture, we could be accused of overt fundamentalism or even bibliolatry. But such an accusation would be plausible only if we did not examine the nature of the Bible itself more carefully.

> We properly read Scripture within the believing community, informed by the tradition of that community. We interpret individual texts in the light of their place in the Bible as a whole.
>
> We are aided by scholarly inquiry and personal insight, under the guidance of the Holy Spirit. As we work with each text, we take into account what we have been able to learn about the original context and intention of that text. In this undertaking we draw upon the careful historical, literary, and textual studies of recent years, which have enriched our understanding of the Bible.[5]

According to this statement, there are four facets that must be considered in the "doing" of theology: scripture, tradition, reason, and experience. It is important to note that these four facets exist in close relationship in the Bible—they have not been arbitrarily determined. The above statement continues: "In recognizing the interrelationship and inseparability of the four basic resources for theological understanding, we are following a model which is present in the biblical text itself." [6]

An example of this biblical model of interpretation is found in Genesis. If one reads the story of the Tower of Babel (Gen. 11:1-9) as a story removed from anything that precedes or follows it in the book of Genesis, one could conclude that the God in that story is a fearful God, jealous of human ingenuity and powerful enough to stop attempts to usurp divine prerogatives by causing the people to speak different languages. However, because we are concerned with seeing the Bible's several contexts, both ancient and modern, this reading is not adequate. Since at least the time of Gerhard von Rad, it has been noted that this story is the final rumbling of the avalanche of sin begun in the garden in chapter three of Genesis. [7] The question to ask is this: Will God leave the human creation alone and isolated one from another, without hope of redemption? The call of Abraham in chapter 12 is a resounding No! God is still at work for the salvation of the people. The Bible points here to a tradition of its own by placing the story of the Tower of Babel in a particular context. To read the story out of that context is to deny the tradition's placement of the story and thus to misread the story. Reading about the God of Genesis 1–11 and about God's relationship to the creation provides clues to a fuller and more appropriate reading of the passage. Our reason ties these various experiences of a tradition-directed reading into a coherent portrait of a God who loves the creation and simply cannot let it fall to its own destruction. Scripture, then, can serve as source and criterion for theology *only* when we remember its diversity and own demand that we employ the resources of tradition, reason, and experience to interpret it aright.

If all scripture is a necessary, but not a sufficient, criterion for the task of thinking theologically, then why should narrative be given pride of place? It is obvious that much of scripture is hardly narrative in form. Yet I argue that narrative is central to the Bible's own interests in communicating its message and therefore calls preachers to employ it as one important means for communicating to their modern congregations.

Although this book focuses its attention on the Hebrew Bible, I assume that the majority of my readers are Christians. Yet a statement previously quoted referred to God's self-disclosure in Jesus Christ and in the pilgrimage of Israel. Hence, I will use examples from both testaments to demonstrate my thesis: *that narrative is central to the Bible's own interests in communicating its message.*

The Call of Moses

As Israel kept its memories of its relationship with God alive, first orally and then in written expression, those who chose narrative as their primary mode of communication were bound, by the very nature of the narrative medium, to discover God as a character in those narratives. Inevitably, they suggested that God is a lover of the divine story, a story in which God is the chief actor. The relationship between these narrators and their God, however, far transcended that of character and author. This God demonstrated a deep love and passion for the divine story but also called Israel to account for its *shared* story—the story of God it shared within its community and the story it shared with God about God. God is described as having a profound investment in that story and thus is a *storied* God, as well as a raconteur—a lover of and teller of the story. The human narrators recognized that the story itself was their way to keep the relationship between God and themselves alive. But more than that, they recognized and affirmed that God, like themselves, found the clearest and most memorable expression of the eternal divine-human relationship in the telling and the hearing of stories.

Although this divine-human relationship was founded and maintained by narrative, Israel did not rely on narrative alone to plumb the depths of this relationship. They found that any one genre was inadequate to express God's commands and grace for them as well as for their varied response to God. Hence they sang and wrote psalms, uttered and codified laws, reflected on experience and penned proverbs, brooded on life and produced Ecclesiastes, defied the very basic traditions of their own past and

21

offered the book of Job to the world, expressed dissatisfaction with the religion that had once helped to make them whole and spoke the poetry of the prophets. Yet, before all these, there was a story that helped to create and sustain the relationship and inform and shape all other expressions of it: the story of Moses.

Moses stands at the very heart of what has been called the master story of Judaism.[8] When Jews tell Moses' story, they announce the center of their tradition. The call to Moses from the midst of the unquenchable fire is the heart of this central story. God, as the divine storyteller, bids Moses, the chosen one, to tell the divine story to maintain the divine-human relationship that God established with humanity at the beginning of creation. As we hear the story again, we will focus on what God asks Moses to do, how Moses responds to this request, what sort of God makes this request, and, most important for our interest, how Moses ultimately learns how he is to communicate with God and other human beings.

The story begins with Moses fleeing Egypt, running for his very life from an enraged pharaoh, his adopted grandfather, who is after him for killing an Egyptian overseer. Moses finds his way to the land of Midian where he rescues the seven daughters of the local priest from a group of rowdy shepherds and later marries one of the seven, Zipporah by name, who soon bears him a son. Although Moses is "content to live" there (Exod. 2:21), he names his son Gershom, which means "sojourner there."

One day Moses is pasturing Jethro's flocks near God's mountain, Horeb. Suddenly, Moses sees a burning bush—a common occurrence in the tinder-dry deserts of Midian—but incredibly, this bush burns but is not consumed. God calls to Moses from the bush and is immediately revealed to us as a clever storyteller (Exod. 3:7-10). Nine times in four verses, God uses first-person verbs and pronouns to announce the divine story and plan. God has seen, heard, known, come to deliver, and God will bring them out. The overwhelming divine story is offered to the shepherd as a fait accompli: *I* have seen, and *I* will do! Then the first-person flood is dammed abruptly by the first use of the second person. "I will send *you*," says God, and Moses the observer is suddenly transformed into Moses the actor. God, the raconteur, has cleverly seduced Moses into the grandeur of the story and has pulled him to the very center of the matter. It is a delightful bit of rhetorical trickery that catches Moses completely off guard.

Chosen as chief actor in the divine drama of salvation, Moses attempts to wriggle out of the part by giving five increasingly lame excuses. Desperately he progresses from "Who me?" to "Who are you?" to "Nobody will believe this!" to "I am a very poor speaker!" Finally, after his paltry arguments are rejected by a God who will brook no argument, he blurts out the last cry of one who is trapped and knows it. "O, my Lord! Please send whomever you send!" (Exod. 4:13) The New Revised Standard Version—"O, my LORD please send someone else"—is not incorrect, but it loses some of the false acceptance that the more literal reading holds. "Whatever you want, God!" says Moses, but what he means is "Choose anyone but me!" God hears the underlying meaning and is rightly furious.

The final emphasis in the story is on telling. God singles out Aaron, Moses's brother, as a good speaker and, in typical story fashion, tells Moses that Aaron is coming even now to meet him, filled with a "glad heart." Finally, God gives Moses clear instructions about his task.

> You will speak to him, and you will put the words in his mouth. I will be with your mouth and his mouth. I will teach both of you what you will do. He shall speak for you to the people; he will be a mouth for you, and you shall be for him as God. (Exod. 4:15-16, author's translation)

"You shall be for him as God." This is what Moses is to be—the mouth of God for Aaron and ultimately for the people. How is the mouth of God to be characterized? It is primarily the mouth of a storyteller, one who loves the stories of God and who tells them to the people. Of course, Moses does much more than tell stories, but his leadership is based on the great actions of God, which are recounted in narrative form.

Moses ultimately becomes God's chief storyteller. Through his persistence in the telling, the people find their freedom. In fact, Moses learns to become such a good storyteller, in the image of his God, that later, when the people have once again fallen away from the desires of God by their worshiping a golden calf, he finds himself confronted by the mighty anger of God. God urges Moses to move out of the way of the divine fury, because God is fed up with the Israelites and has decided to destroy them (Exod. 32:10). But God's own promise to be "with" the mouth of Moses is fulfilled as Moses the reluctant teller becomes Moses the raconteur in order to save his people from the very God who called them. In three mini-stories, Moses convinces God not to destroy the people (Exod. 32:12-13).

Moses learned his lessons well. When God first spoke to him, God told the divine story and bid Moses to become a teller of that story. In the very face of God, Moses becomes what God has promised he would be: a possessor of the mouth of God—a teller of the divine story. God is glad to hear the story told by the chosen one, and the result of the telling is that the people are spared; the mind of God is changed by Moses's telling (Exod. 32:14). The basic function of the story is to effect a change of heart and mind, for such is the power of this story—power that can change the very heart of God.

The Legacy of Moses the Storyteller

Moses is the paradigm case of the call of God to be tellers of the divine story, but the call does not stop with Moses. As illustrated by scripture, to tell the story is what God continually calls the chosen to do. Moses, of course, sets the pattern.

In Exodus 13:13-15, the irrevocable relationship between liturgy and the story of God is established, a relationship that persists in Judaism and Christianity today.

> Every first-born of an ass you shall redeem with a lamb. If you will not redeem it, you shall break its neck. Every first born among your sons you shall redeem. Whenever your son asks you in future, "What is all this?" you shall say to him, "With a powerful hand Yahweh brought us out of Egypt, out of the house of slavery. When pharaoh stubbornly refused to send us out, Yahweh killed all of the first-born of the land of Egypt from human to cattle. That is why I sacrifice to Yahweh all males that first open the womb, but all my first-born sons I redeem."

24

It has long been recognized that this particular concern for appropriate sacrifice was a later addition to the story of the Exodus narrative, although the roots of the practice itself may be very old. What is important for this argument, however, is the fact that Moses is still seen by the tradition to be primarily concerned with the transmission of the story of Yahweh. The very purpose of the sacrificial practice is rooted in the great story of the Exodus. Without the narrative there would be no reason for celebrating the ritual; the ritual is designed to enshrine the narrative in acts that refer directly to that narrative. Moses enjoins his followers to right sacrifice, and at the same time, urges them to transmit clearly the reason for offering sacrifice—namely, the telling of the story of the Exodus.

This connection between the narrative and sacrifice is further demonstrated in those significant places in the Hebrew Bible when offerings are brought to Yahweh. In Deuteronomy 26:5-11, all true worshipers of Yahweh are commanded to take an offering of the first fruits of the harvest to Yahweh's sanctuary and, upon presenting it to the officiating priest, are asked to recite the narrative credo of Israel. The credo consists of references to a "wandering" (or "perishing") Aramean who descended into Egypt to deliver God's chosen people who, though at first few in number, became a great and mighty nation. The credo continues by telling how they were afflicted, how they cried out to God, and how they were delivered by God and brought to the land whose fruits are presented as a living reminder of the narrative. As the priest receives the fruits, the narrative recital is to begin (Deut. 26:4-5); the fruits accompany and symbolize the narrative of Israel, just as bread and wine accompany and symbolize the passion narrative in the Christian Eucharist.

The use of pronouns in the credo clearly illustrates the important role of the narrative. The recital of the credo begins with a third-person reference to the Aramean who is "my father" and who becomes a great and mighty nation in Egypt. But the third-person references become first-person references beginning with verse six. "The Egyptians treated *us* harshly," and "*we* cried out to Yahweh" who saw "*our* affliction, *our* toil, *our* oppression." Yahweh brought *us* out of Egypt, "brought *us* into this place and gave *us* this land." In effect, the recital of the credo moves away from a simple enumeration of the events in the past to a realization that the events are for *me*. In fact, says the worshiper, the ancient story is *my* story; I appropriate it for myself by learning it, telling it, and celebrating it through my worship.

A well-known rabbinic story reinforces this point. When the Baal Shem Tov saw evil threatening the Jews, he would go to a certain place in the forest to meditate. There he would light a fire and say a certain prayer. A miracle would happen and the evil would be averted. When his disciple, the Magid of Mezritch, found himself in a similar fearful circumstance, he would go to the same place in the forest and say, "Master of the universe, I do not know how to light the fire, but I am still able to say the prayer." The miracle would soon occur. When *his* disciple, Rabbi Moshe-leib of Sasov, found himself in a similar fearful circumstance, he would go to the same place in the forest and say, "Master of the universe, I do not know how to light the fire, nor do I know the prayer, but I am at the right place, and that must be sufficient." It would be, and the miracle would soon occur. Then one day his disciple, Rabbi Israel of Rizhyn, found himself in a similar fearful circumstance. He sat at home, his head in his hands, and said, "Master of the universe, I am unable to light the fire, I do not know the prayer, nor can I find the right place in the forest. All I can do is tell the story, and that must be sufficient." It was.[9]

Other Calls to Tell the Story

In addition to its role in worship, storytelling serves other functions in the Hebrew Bible. In Deuteronomy 6:20-24, the reader is again commanded to tell the story of the Exodus, but this time the demand is made in the context of teaching rather than worship. The reader is to tell the story in response to the child's question about the meaning of the Ten Commandments. This question is identical to the question asked in Exodus 13:14—"What does it mean?"—but here the context is the commandments rather than the offering of first fruits. The response also is basically the same: The meaning of the "testimonies, and statues, and ordinances" is the story of God's actions in Egypt.

Because all the pronouns used in the recital of the story are in the first-person plural, we may draw the same conclusion here as we drew in our examination of Exodus 13. The narrative recital is the underlying meaning of the commandments offered to the people from the sacred mountain, just as that same recital was the underlying meaning of the offering of the first fruits. If one is to understand either the commandments or the offering of the first fruits to Yahweh, one must understand and tell the story of the activity of Yahweh—done not only for those so long ago but also performed on behalf of all those who know and tell the story.

The narrative recital also finds its way into the psalmic literature of the people of Israel. Psalms 105, 135, and 136 offer examples of the narrative recital turned to song. Even in these poems, the purpose of the narrative recital is to affirm basic insights about Yahweh and to bring about the affirmation and transformation of the people. In Psalm 105, the covenant that God offers to the people is best expressed when the narrative recital is sung (vv. 9-42). In Psalm 135, the psalmist tells us that "the Lord is great" and then makes this evident through a recital that begins with creation (vs.7) and concludes with an assault on idolatry (vv. 15-18). In Psalm 136, the very reason for the repeated refrain "God's steadfast love endures forever" is the narrative recital, which it so memorably punctuates, from creation (vv. 5-9) to God's miraculous gift of food for all (v. 25). (For other examples of narrative recitals, see Exodus 15, Joshua 24, I Samuel 12, and Nehemiah 9.)

The Dangers of Losing the Story

We have examined several ways in which the knowledge and the telling of the story of God have played a central role in the ongoing lives of faith of the people of Israel. The examples have come from various historical periods of Israel's life, indicating the ubiquitous nature of the concern for transmitting the narrative of God. Throughout Israel's history the story has had the power to transform, to urge choice, and to command praise. But as the prophet Jeremiah asks: What happens if the story should disappear from the people?[10]

In chapter two of Jeremiah's prophecy, he indicts his generation's immediate forebears in ringing words, which he claims come directly from their God. First he accuses those who traveled through the wilderness of rejecting God.

> What sin did your forebears find in me
>   that they went so far away from me?
> They went after emptiness and became empty. (Jer. 2:4)

This general charge that the people of the wilderness "went away" from God, seeking "emptiness," is made more specific in verse 6.

> They did not say, "Where is Yahweh,
>   who brought us out of the land of Egypt,
>   who led us in the wilderness, in a land of
>   deserts and pits,
>   a land of drought and darkness,
>   a land where none may pass through,
>   where no one lives?" (Jer. 2:6)

For Jeremiah, "to go far away from God" is to cease the recital of God's actions. One sign that God is being forgotten and rejected is the absence of the recital of God's activity on behalf of the people. The result of this refusal to speak the story is emptiness. But the people of the wilderness generation are not the only ones who forgot the story or who refused to tell it. Jeremiah shifts his accusations from the wilderness generation to his own generation as the pronouns switch to the second person.

> I brought you into a plentiful land
>   to eat fine fruits.
> But when you entered, you defiled my land,
>   and made my inheritance an abomination. (Jer. 2:7)

Again Jeremiah begins his attack with a general charge, speaking of defilement and abomination, and again he quickly specifies his charges.

> The priests did not say, "Where is Yahweh?"
>   Those who interpret the teaching did not know me.
> The shepherds [i.e., the rulers] rebelled against me. (Jer. 2:8)

Here Jeremiah accuses the contemporary priests and leaders of the nation with the same charge he leveled at the people of the wilderness: they did not say, "Where is Yahweh?" The question of verse 8, then, is a shortened version of the longer charge of verses 6-7. The problem is the same in both cases: The story of God is no longer known or recited, especially by those who are charged with its preservation and transmission.

The terrible results of this loss, which is nothing less than a "change of gods" (vs. 11), are spelled out in verse 13.

> Surely, two evils have been done by my people:
>   Me they have abandoned,
> the source of living waters,
>   in order to dig cisterns for themselves,
> broken cisterns, which can hold no water. (Jer. 2:13)

To abandon the story of Yahweh is to abandon Yahweh, the source of living waters. After this abandonment, the next evil is to rely on one's own resources—to dig for one's own water. But without God, the human cisterns are broken and can hold no water. Without the story of Yahweh, there can be no knowledge of Yahweh, and hence there can be no real life; there can be only a community that thinks self-reliance leads to life. But as Jeremiah's prophecy portrays in detail, self-reliance leads only to death.

The examples from Exodus, Deuteronomy, Psalms, and Jeremiah should be sufficient proof of the crucial nature of the recital of the narrative of God for the Hebrew Bible. God is a raconteur who bids the chosen ones to join the band of storytellers. To tell that story is to "be as God," as God tells Moses in Exodus 4:16. The result of the telling is that the presence of God is remembered with a power that can transform, command praise, and change the very heart of God. To forget or deny that story leads to loss of the God revealed in it—a loss that results in decline and death. For the Hebrew Bible, to tell the story is the most urgent activity of the faithful. Theologically speaking, the Hebrew Bible *insists* that all of God's people are charged to become tellers of the story of God.

Narrative and the New Testament

Just as narrative plays an important role in the Hebrew Bible, so narrative is of great significance in the New Testament. Johann Metz says that the basic datum of the New Testament, the cross and the resurrection of Jesus, "has a narrative structure." [11] That is, the early Christian communities chose to relate the memory of the death and resurrection of the one they called Savior in the form of a narrative, rather than as a creed or cultic poem. Although both the creed and cultic poem were developed early in the tradition, the basic "shape" of the recounting of the crucifixion and resurrection was a story. Even Paul, who tended to be influenced less by narrative forms than by philosophical and Greek rhetorical genres, chose the narrative form to communicate the resurrection of Jesus in his first letter to the Corinthians (I Cor. 15:3-9)—which possibly is the earliest form in which we have such a report. The Gospels, generated in four diverse communities, also take the form of a narrative.

As Metz affirms, the narrative structure of cross and resurrection serves as the basic story of the gospel which urges believers to a faith in the "redemption of history and in the new man (and woman)." [12] This means that the central story of the gospel subverts those who decide that human suffering and hopelessness are the final words of human existence. Such a faith, then, can generate powerfully liberating stories that can transform hearers into doers. One such liberating story altered forever the life of Peter. His change from the defeated disciple who wept by the fire (Luke 26:62), to the great preacher of the resurrected Christ (Acts 2) was accomplished by his belief in and powerful recounting of the story of Jesus Christ. As in Exodus 13:14 and Deuteronomy 6:20, Peter tells the story in response to the recurring question, "What does it mean?" (Acts 2:12). Thus, the ancient pattern of the Hebrew Bible is repeated. When the hearer wants to know what the actions of God are and what they mean, the speaker responds by telling the story of the actions of God.

The parables offer other examples of this "central subversive story of the gospel." Sallie McFague says that the parables of Jesus are in reality "extended metaphors."[13]

30

A parable is not an allegory, where the meaning is extrinsic to the story, nor is it an example story where, as in the story of the Good Samaritan, the total meaning is within the story. Rather, as an extended metaphor, the meaning is found only *within* the story itself although it is not exhausted *by* that story.[14]

One cannot extrapolate from the parable a "point" or an abstract concept without destroying the very function that the parable as extended metaphor is trying to serve. If I boil the parable down into a point or points, I have at the same time made it impossible for the parable itself to "reveal a new setting for ordinary life."[15] In short, the parables must be read first and last as stories, if their peculiar power to engage the unfamiliar (for example, the realm of God) by means of the familiar (vineyards, robbers, or wayward children) is to be released to the hearers.

Because parables were one of the chief vehicles of Jesus' preaching, and because the parables are not merely earthly messages with heavenly meaning but rather are complex and irreducible works of narrative art, we have further reason for pursuing a narrative homiletics. Recent scholarly work has examined the parables as stories, with questions of plot, structure, and characterization clearly at the forefront of the discussions.[16]

As we have seen, narrative is a prominent genre in both the Hebrew Bible and the New Testament. In both testaments, one important mode of communication urged on all who would claim to communicate the power of the word of God is the narrative mode. Because the basic content of the biblical message so often is couched in narrative and transmitted in narrative, those who would understand and communicate that message are urged to explore a narrative homiletics. Such a homiletics becomes, then, not only acceptable or respectable; it becomes a mandate from the biblical text.

A NARRATIVE QUALITY OF EXPERIENCE

I have attempted to establish the case that the Bible is both the chief warrant for a theology of narrative homiletics and the persuading agent that urges us to pursue a narrative homiletics. Can we also find another warrant for a narrative homiletics in the character of our own experience of reality? In other words, do the Bible's urgings toward narrative communication find a world of human experience in which to communicate that is itself characterized by a narrative shape? If so, it can be said that not only are the "mode and matter" of our preaching well served by narrative, but even the milieu where that preaching is done—with its own possible narrative shape—is a uniquely appropriate place for the reception of such narrative.

As we begin the discussion, a careful distinction must be made between reality and experience. I have suggested that we explore the possibility that the contexts of our narrative preaching— preaching itself already characterized by a distinctively narrative mode and matter—might also possess their own narrative quality and thus offer narrative preaching an especially receptive soil in which to plant its work. I do not mean that reality itself has some sort of narrative form. Such a claim could be only purely metaphysical and would lead us into areas that I will leave for others to pursue. I mean to affirm Stephen Crites' claim that our *experience* of reality has a narrative form.[17] According to Crites, "When we speak to or of what is immediately real to us we tell stories and fragments of stories. 'Ordinary language' is largely made up of the sorts of locutions we employ in telling stories."[18] Thus, according to Crites, there is a "narrative quality of experience."[19]

Crites identifies three areas of experience that make up what he calls the narrative quality of experience. The first is "sacred story." By sacred story he means those generally ancient "mythopoeic stories" sung or danced which are "anonymous and communal." These are to be distinguished from legends or myths, which we are able to read in ancient texts. He says, "Such stories, and the symbolic worlds they project, are not like monuments that men [and women] behold, but like dwelling-places. People live in them."[20] Perhaps one could call these oral stories the stories behind those stories that can be read. These sacred stories, "though not directly told," nonetheless seem to be narrative in form. That is, they are "moving forms, . . . which inform people's sense of the story of which their own lives are a part, of the moving course of their own action and experience."[21] These ancient stories form the bedrock of the communal experience of those who embrace them as descriptive *and* prescriptive for their lives together. Because they possess an inherent narrative quality, these stories infuse that narrative quality into the very core of human experience.

Arising from these sacred stories are what Crites calls "mundane stories," written expressions of the sacred stories which "may carry the authority of scripture for the people who understand their own stories in relation to them."[22] These latter, and temporally later written expressions form the second component of the three-pronged narrative quality of experience. Mundane stories are those we can read and examine by using the traditional tools of narrative analysis: the examination of word-choice, scenes, sequence of events within a plot, and so forth. These mundane stories form the articulation and clarification of the sense of the world that was originally formed by the sacred stories. As Crites explains, an obvious relationship exists between these two kinds of stories: "Between sacred and mundane stories there is distinction without separation. From the sublime to the ridiculous, all a people's mundane stories are implicit in its sacred story, and every mundane story takes soundings in the sacred story."[23]

Crites does not prove that the sacred story is, in fact, narrative; he merely assumes that it is because of the obvious narrative nature of the mundane stories that arise from it. Furthermore, Crites does not claim that the convergence of art and experience, which yields narrative in the form of mundane stories, always "occurs in narrative form alone."[24] His point is similar to one that I have been making: narrative is a significant genre of human expression, but not the only one. Even in cultures such as ours, whose fiction (i.e. mundane stories) often is an attempt to break the tyranny of the patterns of narrativity,[25] the sacred story is still very much alive and is attempting to reassert itself, albeit in ever new and sometimes almost unrecognizable forms. As Crites says, "Break the story to tell a truer story!"[26] However the narrative appears, either in traditional forms or in forms designed to annihilate the tradition, a basic narrativity of experience is assumed.

The third component of the narrative quality of experience is the "inner form of experience." According to Crites, "Between sacred story and mundane stories there is a mediating form: the form of the experiencing consciousness itself." [27] By drawing upon

Augustine's reflections on memory and time in his *Confessions,* Crites insists that "my" experiencing consciousness is a combination of three facets. The first is my present existence, which is provided needed depth by the second facet: my memory. Memory, the content of my experience, makes my present what it is. That memory is coupled with my anticipation of the future—the third facet—which serves as the trajectory of my hoped-for or feared actions still to come.

Crites explains that in the complex interaction of past, present, and future, my experiencing consciousness can unify these three modalities as well as distinguish the three. It can do this because that experiencing assumes a narrative form. He says that "narrative alone can contain the full temporality of experience in the unity of form."[28] Without the moving quality of the narrative, I could not hold the competing modes of past, present, and future in tension within my consciousness, nor could I apprehend in their narrative fullness either the sacred story or the mundane stories that arise from it. Crites concludes that each of these three components of the narrative quality of experience both reflects and affects the others.[29]

Crites' work is important to our exploration of the possibility of a narrative homiletics because it affirms that the biblical stories are those mundane stories that clearly show a narrative face. They show this narrative face, Crites explains, because the sacred story that underlies them—the experience with the divine that characterizes the Hebrew tradition, for example—also has a narrative form. Crites suggests that because our own experiencing consciousness is also narratively shaped, we best apprehend the sacred story and its mundane story offspring in the form of narrative. Narrative, therefore, is constitutive of both the biblical tradition—which is the foundation of our theological reflection—and our experience of that tradition, as well as the rest of our experience.

In conclusion, the theological significance of a narrative homiletics is indicated from the primary warrant for any homiletics, the Bible, and from the very ways in which we experience the narratives of the Bible and our lives—which are, specifically, narrative ways. Theologically speaking, a narrative homiletics is important if we are to take seriously significant portions of the biblical tradition and their powerful communication and reception in our congregations. There is, however, a more practical reason for the telling of narratives. In a world where narrative is so basic to cultures and their expressions, the controlling narratives of a given culture must be identified and addressed if that culture is to undergo what religious people have long called conversion.

> If experience has the narrative quality attributed to it here, not only our self-identity but the empirical and moral cosmos in which we are conscious of living is implicit in our multidimensional story. It therefore becomes evident that a conversion or a social revolution that actually transforms consciousness requires a traumatic change in a man's [and a woman's] story. The stories within which he [she] has awakened to consciousness must be undermined, and in the identification of his [her] personal story through a new story, both the drama of 3his [her] experience and his (her) style of action must be reoriented. Conversion is reawakening, a second awakening of consciousness.[30]

For real conversion to occur, nothing less than a "traumatic change in a person's story" is required. Thus, a narrative homiletics holds the possibility for a "traumatic change of story" and a chance for real conversion.

NARRATIVE PREACHING

A REVOLUTION IN PREACHING

The shape of preaching is open to radical reorientation now, however, simply because the transformed sensibilities resulting from cultural shifts through the twentieth century no longer give wholesale sanction to the assumptions underlying the argument form. . . . Regardless of changing theologies and varying cultures through the centuries, preaching mostly assumed a debater's stance. . . . The Greeks have stolen into homiletical Troy and still reign.[1]

Why should the multitude of forms and moods within Biblical literature and the multitude of needs in the congregation be brought together in one unvarying mold, and that copied from Greek rhetoricians of centuries ago? An unnecessary monotony results, but more profoundly, there is an inner conflict between the content of the sermon and its form.[2]

The White middle-class church suffers today from the fact that its leadership has been taught to scoff at and war against the "less intellectual" world view of the average member. . . . Too many have sacrificed too much trying to deal consciously and intellectually with that which was not naturally amenable to such processes.[3]

There is a revolution occurring in the field of preaching. Hardly a volume on the subject of homiletics has appeared in the past fifteen years that has not contained such challenging passages. In the minds of these homileticians and their colleagues, something is amiss in the pulpits of the late twentieth century. What is perceived to be wrong may be summarized in two ways.

First, the basic tool of preaching, the Bible, is seriously misused. In the previously quoted books, each of the authors discusses at length how the Bible has functioned and continues to function for most contemporary preachers. The method employed has been called *distillation*.[4] When using this method, all biblical texts are treated essentially in the same way: The text is read in search of themes or points that are then ordered on the basis of a traditional model of argumentation. An "old friend" named "three points and a poem," suddenly rears its hoary head. Whenever this "old friend" is mentioned in a room full of preachers, peals of laughter ring out, somehow implying that we don't know this "old friend" anymore. My own experience of hearing sermons preached in pulpits and classrooms suggests that the laughter is reflective of embarrassed familiarity rather than satiric rejection.

The ubiquitous presence of this "old friend" suggests the second problem identified by many homileticians: The preaching experience frequently is argumentative in nature. Richard Eslinger describes it this way: "Burdened with a rationalist bias, the old homiletic is based on a static model of argumentation derived from Hellenistic rhetoric."[5] This kind of preaching— sometimes called discursive, didactic, or conceptual—"makes points." The sermon announces a topic or theme and then attempts to prove that this topic or theme is important and worthy of time devoted to it in the worship service.[6] The style of this kind of sermon usually is deductive; the announced topic is followed by a summary conclusion. The argumentation is not necessarily syllogistic (A and B and therefore C) but may be loosely Hegelian (thesis-antithesis-synthesis), simply descriptive with no real attempt to argue the point at all ("We know this by experience" or "We really are like Samson"), or primarily linear (taking its cues from the classroom lecture or the debater's tournament).

This is not to say that argumentative preaching is no longer desirable or effective in our time. Effective preaching in the mode of argument has been done, is being done, and will continue to be done as long as preachers preach. The purpose of this book is not to reject argumentative preaching; rather, the purpose of this book is to offer preachers important alternatives so that their preaching does not harden into a dulling "sameness." A steady diet of discursive sermons based on linear logic and argumentation can lead to stagnation for both preacher and hearer. If the congregation is already certain about how the sermon will go before the preacher stands up to give it, then the sense of anticipation is dulled and expectations will be low. But if the congregation is not certain what the preacher will do, and if the preacher has prepared the members to expect the unexpected, then their anticipation will be heightened and their ability to receive the message will be enhanced by the element of surprise lurking in the preacher's words.

I have argued theologically, both from the perspective of the biblical narratives themselves and from the perspective of the narrative quality of experience, that preachers who would preach from narrative texts are urged to explore the possibility of a narrative homiletics. Such a homiletics is more than a fad or a homiletical trick; it is a fully appropriate, highly significant means to communicate the Word of God that has come to us in the form of narrative. There are, however, more practical reasons for the value of a narrative homiletics. Some of these considerations are evident in the practical effects that occur when choosing a particular type of narrative sermon.

PREACHING THE STORY

A speaker must always subordinate narration to the object of his [her] discourse, the conviction or persuasion which he [she] wishes to effect. He [she] must not elaborate or enlarge upon some narrative merely because it is in itself interesting or follow the story step by step according to its own laws.[7]

That statement was written by John Broadus more than one hundred years ago, but it still represents a widespread understanding of how a story is to be used in a sermon. Here are the implications of the statement:

1. Narration is always to be subordinate to the "object of the discourse." Therefore, narration is seen to be adjunct to the primary

[Handwritten margin note: cf sermon on Ruth — p. 93 "idea of Ruth as God — is the persuation which he wishes to effect.]

task of the sermon, which is said to be the presentation of the "object." The implication is that narrative is to be kept under tight control so that this "object" is not overwhelmed by it.

2. The "object" of the sermon is "conviction or persuasion," and narration must not be allowed to short-circuit that overriding concern.

3. The preacher must not elaborate on the narration so as to make it too interesting. The object presumably will be swept away by the congregation's interest, and conviction and persuasion thereby will be diluted.

4. The story must not be followed "step by step according to its own laws." Again the implication is that the story, if told according to its own laws, will overpower the object, and the sermon will be reduced to some form of entertainment.

Although Broadus goes on to urge preachers to narrate "those beautiful and sacred stories" more often than they do, it is clear from his extended statement that he is concerned about the misuse of those stories in preaching. His statement contains a telling irony. If the goal of preaching is conviction and persuasion, and if the biblical narratives possess the possibility of overwhelming this homiletical "object" because they are so interesting, would it not be possible to harness that interest-producing power to the goal of the stated object? Why must the interest of the narrative speak *against* the object of conviction and persuasion? We of the late twentieth century hear in Broadus's concern a Victorian prejudice against unruly entertainment invading the sacred precincts of the sermon. But regardless of his motives, he was uncomfortable with the power of narrative. Indeed, his preaching textbook *On the Preparation and Delivery of Sermons* contains fewer than five pages on narrative or story. Because Broadus's textbook recently has been updated and reprinted in a fourth edition, his continuing influence among certain preachers is assured.

Though it is not my intent to give a complete history of the rise of story preaching, it is instructive to see how influential textbooks have treated the subject. A generation of seminarians has been served by H. Grady Davis's *Design for Preaching*, now thirty years old. That it is still in print indicates its continuing influence. Davis offers these insightful and prophetic words about preaching and story:

> A sermon idea may take the form of a narrative of events, persons, action, and words. The distinguishing feature of this form is that the idea is embodied in a structure of events and persons, rather than in a structure of verbal generalizations, whether assertions or questions.[8]

Note that Davis says that the idea is "embodied" in the narrative structure, not "embedded" in it. Davis implies here that by using a narrative structure, one does not merely clothe an idea in a different dress; rather, an idea embodied by narrative is, in a real sense, different from that same idea presented in a "structure of verbal generalizations." "Since form does its work immediately and at deeper levels than logic, persuades directly and silently as it were, form has an importance second only to that of thought itself."[9] Davis's brief section on narrative concludes with these words, which could have been written today:

> After all this is said, however, it remains a fact that too little use is made of narrative in contemporary preaching, and that on rare occasions a good telling of the biblical story would be more effective than the best exposition of general ideas of which the preacher is capable.[10]

No recent book on the theory or practice of homiletics fails to discuss the importance of story. James Cox, for example, says in his textbook *Preaching*, "The preacher who takes account of this narrative quality of the Christian faith and who proceeds homiletically from this fact is the preacher who will be heard."[11] Likewise, in his brief book *Preaching*, Dean Lueking writes, "It clutters the way when the preacher falls into the habit of saying, 'This point reminds me of a story.' That's needless. The point is not that the preacher is reminded. The point is in the story itself."[12]

Other noteworthy scholars have done much to fuel the interest in narrative preaching as well. In his Beecher lectures, *Telling the Truth*, Frederick Buechner announces in memorable prose the poetic quality of the Bible's story: "With his [her] fabulous tale to proclaim, the preacher is called in his [her] turn to stand up in his [her] pulpit as fabulist extraordinary, to tell the truth of the Gospel in its highest and wildest and holiest sense."[13] Similarly, Fred Craddock has continually urged preachers not to neglect the power of the metaphor, especially as it is found in narrative. In *Overhearing the Gospel*, he writes, "Narratives reproduce and recreate events, with characters developing and events unfolding, and the teller reexperiencing while narrating. This reexperiencing is the source of the emotive and imaginative power in the telling."[14] Finally, Henry Mitchell, an African-American preacher, has tried to convey—particularly to white preachers—just how the black preacher has been nourished and sustained by the biblical narrative. In *Recovery of Preaching* he argues for the narrative method as first choice.

> After all the issues were faced and adequate freedom from Western models of communication was achieved, my classes have agreed with me that no other form should be used in preference to a good story. When one uses an intellectual argument or essay form, it ought to be either an adjunct to a shorter story or a choice growing out of the fact that one has no story suitable for that particular gospel idea.[15]

With Mitchell, we come 180 degrees from John Broadus, who claimed that narrative should be used carefully and only as an adjunct to the primary "object" of the sermon. Mitchell reverses this order and says that the narrative is the primary form, whereas argument has become the adjunct to it! Mitchell is certainly witness to the homiletical revolution that has taken place in our time.

Given the fact that there is much interest in story preaching, two questions must be addressed to aid the preacher in exploring the possibilities of narrative preaching. First, what is the definition of a "narrative sermon," and second, what are the strengths and weaknesses of this type of preaching?

TYPES OF NARRATIVE SERMONS

Pure Narrative

A *pure narrative* sermon is just that: a narrative. Or as Jensen says, "The story is the preaching itself."[16] In other words, a pure narrative sermon is a story—no more and no less. The story may be embellished in its detail and dressed up in its execution, but it is still only a story. *Pure* simply means that the story is in no sense explained to the hearer, or commented on, outside the bounds of the narrative. In such a sermon, no introduction or conclusion outside of the story is used. The story's introduction is the sermon's introduction; the story's conclusion is the sermon's conclusion. In a pure narrative sermon, the storyteller should allow the Bible's own way of expressing its concerns to inform directly his or her way of expressing those concerns. Thus, in matters of both form and content, a pure narrative sermon tries to mirror *in detail* the Bible's story.

This does not mean, of course, that the storyteller merely tells the Bible's story word for word, or simply reads it dramatically. A pure narrative sermon does not hamstring the storyteller's imagination when it comes to contemporizing the Bible's word for the modern congregation. Nor does this mean that narrative preaching is old-style expository preaching in modern dress. Rather, a pure narrative sermon does not move through the text line by line, offering comments on matters of exegetical niceties, but it *tells* the story by recounting details provided by a careful reading. My sermon "The Best Laugh of All" (chap. 4) is an attempt at a pure narrative sermon.

Frame Narrative

Sometimes a preacher may wish to provide some sort of introduction to the narrative in order to help the congregation understand the significance of the narrative—as "discovered" by the preacher. Such a device might be used if the story is unusually rich in its drama or detail—so rich that the hearer might get lost and thereby lose the thread of its significance. I call this kind of narrative sermon a *frame narrative.* In a frame narrative sermon, the preacher not only may choose to introduce the narrative with some sort of introduction outside of the narrative itself, but he or she also may choose to use a conclusion that focuses the narrative for the congregation. By *focuses the narrative,* I do not mean "explains" the narrative. The story is not an extended illustration for a point to be made at the sermon's end. After telling a story, the preacher should never lean over the pulpit and say, "Now, for all of you who did not get the point of the story I have just told you, here it is." That sort of tactic is *not* a part of narrative preaching, as I am defining it.

The more traditional repertoire of illustrations can be called on to introduce the narrative that is to serve as the bulk of the sermon. We are familiar with these: stories—either personal, biblical, contemporary, or original; quotations—hymns, songs, or words of famous persons; and imaginative—sentences of our own devising. You can add to the list. The idea is to establish, between you and your hearers, the particular reasons why you plan to tell them this extended story. The frame conclusion has the same rationale and takes its material from the same list of illustrations. My sermon "God, The Moabite Widow" (chap. 5) is an attempt at a frame narrative sermon.

Multiple Story Narrative

Bailey

A third kind of narrative sermon is the *multiple story narrative*. In this narrative variety, one biblical story is used to comment directly on another, but the preacher does not comment on either story outside of the bounds provided by that story. The rationale for this kind of narrative sermon is to allow one part of the biblical record to comment on another part, and thus permit the Bible's unique and varied witness to be heard in a richness not available through any one text. If a nonbiblical story is chosen, the sermon would be a frame narrative.

Fictional Narrative

A fourth kind of narrative sermon may be called a *fictional narrative sermon*. In this kind of sermon, the preacher creates a new story inspired by a close reading of the biblical narrative. Sometimes the preacher may discover that the biblical story in its ancient dress does not speak as clearly or forcefully as a contemporary story might. This has prompted some of our greatest authors to tell stories that present the most significant themes of the biblical witness in fresh and often startling ways, which modern hearers, who are perhaps dulled by the familiar formulations of the great old themes, might be enabled to hear these themes again with renewed power.

Preachers are well advised to read and contemplate those authors who, in effect, are attempting to do what preachers are in the business of doing—namely, seeking fresh ways to say familiar things. For example, Flannery O'Connor, an ardent Roman Catholic, spent her tragically brief life trying to confront an increasingly secular society with the awesome mystery of the grace of God. She often chose overtly grotesque forms to effect the confrontation, but her choice was a conscious one. She once said, "I am interested in making up a good case for distortion, as I am coming to believe it is the only way to make people see." [17]

Personal Narrative

In the fifth type of narrative sermon, the preacher's own unique story or personal experience, related as illuminative of the biblical witness, is the bulk of the sermon. By a *personal narrative sermon,* I do not mean that some specific experience of the preacher is used as an illustration of the theme of the day. Rather, one specific experience of the preacher is narrated *in direct response to a specific biblical text,* in order to make that text fresh and new to the hearers. Merely telling "my story" may or may not be a personal narrative sermon as I am defining it. The key is that the experience must be one shared in response to a text. For example, the preacher might relate his or her own conversion experience as it has been illuminated by the conversion experience of Paul. If one of the chief concerns of the preaching task is to share the biblical witness of faith with congregations, then it is incumbent upon the preacher not to use his or her experience merely as an end in itself—regardless of how interesting that experience might be. A personal narrative sermon is offered in response to the Bible's story and should be used only if the Bible's witness is enhanced.

PRESENTING THE STORY

Within each of the five general types of narrative sermons—pure, frame, multiple story, fictional, and personal—there are multiple ways of presenting the material. These "ways" can be called narrative points of view. Perhaps the most obvious way for a preacher to present a story sermon is as a third-person narrator—one who observes the action from the outside but knows everything about the story and chooses to reveal it to the hearer. One might call this *passive* narration, as opposed to an *active* narration in which the preacher becomes a character or takes part in the story in some way. Passive narration is probably the most comfortable and familiar narrative point of view, since it is the one we know best. When we tell jokes, we are usually third-person passive narrators. One advantage of third person is that it is the kind of narrative most often presented in the Bible.

Although third-person narrative is generally a passive point of view, the active third-person narrative is a possible alternative. Whereas the passive third-person narrator tells the story with minimal intrusions, the active third-person narrator tells the story and interacts with the story so that he or she becomes, in effect, part of the story. This can be done in several ways. One could, for example, set up a dialogue with the narrative, asking certain questions of the story to draw out the chosen meanings. Or one might question the narrative as it proceeds, asking questions that the congregation might want to ask of the story. In these two ways and others that the pastor's imagination can create, the story can be illuminated in a fresh way in the active third-person narrative.

First-person narrative point of view is a viable—although more difficult—alternative to the more common third person. In this kind of narration, the preacher *becomes* the character and presents the action and dialogue strictly from the perspective of that character. As one can imagine, the dramatic demands increase in the first-person narrative. The presentation must take with great seriousness the expectations that any audience brings to a dramatic event. This is no time for biblical bathrobe drama! When the preacher assumes a character's role, the congregation has the right to expect him or her to *be* that character. Not only must the preacher be viable dramatically, but he or she also must be true to the story in which the character takes part. If the character is blind (see John 9), then the preacher must narrate as a blind person. If the character is mad (see Mark 5), then the preacher must narrate as if he or she were mad. Not every preacher should attempt first-person narrative preaching; it is demanding physically and emotionally. When done poorly, it can be an embarrassing and humiliating experience for everyone. Worst of all, such an experience does not help to proclaim the gospel. Still, some who are reading this book are capable of powerful first-person preaching, and I urge those individuals to try it.

In addition to choosing a narrative point of view, the preacher who wants to preach narratively should consider using simple props as aids to the sermon. If the story of Moses is the text for the day, a gnarled walking stick can be used to represent the famous rod—if that rod is to play a central role in the telling of the story. If the story of Judas is told, the sound of clinking coins can add power to the visual exchange of money for the life of Jesus. The key is to keep the props simple. If the pulpit becomes a stage, and a robe or suit is exchanged for a costume, the preacher runs the risk of acting rather than preaching. All preachers are actors to some extent, but not all actors are preachers. The creative preacher will think of many ways to aid the presentation of the story.

THE POSSIBILITIES AND PERILS OF NARRATIVE PREACHING

From the discussion thus far, the reader may have discovered the various possibilities and perils of narrative preaching. These possibilities and perils need to be addressed in full if the preacher is to be prepared for the task of narrative preaching. First, let us focus on the possibilities.

In my judgment the primary gift that a preacher and congregation may receive from the narrative style is the basic union of form and content in the sermon. Simply put, a narrative text is wedded to a narrative expression. The best expression of a narrative is a narrative. "Rendering" a narrative into a discursive sermon is to "melt it down," or "turn it into lard." Though I already have addressed this issue in several ways, the union of form and content is so important to the possibility of narrative preaching that I offer one other expression of the significance of this union in the narratives of the Bible.

In this statement from his *Early Christian Rhetoric,* Amos Wilder explains that because the basic form of biblical faith is narrative, to render that narrative into discursive language is to turn it into something it decidedly is not.

> What the early Christian faith meant [and the ancient Hebrew faith as well], therefore, can only be grasped as we attend to its plastic language, giving full heed to what it meant in its original setting. . . . Our congenital modern demand that such language (i.e. that of world redemption, water into wine, Messianic Banquets) be rationalized must be resisted, as well as our readiness to put all such forms of knowing out of court. . . . Transposition of the myth into provisional discursive or existential analogies is desirable provided it be recognized that every such formulation is a poor surrogate and must always again appeal back to the original.[18]

Wilder is making the same point that Henry Mitchell makes in *Recovery of Preaching,* albeit in a different way. The point is this: Not only is discursive rendering of a narrative "unbiblical" because it alters the very form of the Bible's expression, but it also often fails to reach the hearer with the force intended. Narrative language is language that will be heard by our congregations because it is the language that the members know from their own narrative worlds. Furthermore, the language of the Bible, which is far from being alien to our sophisticated world, is closer to our need for "imaginative depth" than we have been able to realize or articulate. Thus, narrative preaching is both truer to the Bible's own narrative in its attention to form, and it holds the possibility of speaking deeply to the needs of late-twentieth-century hearers.

A second possibility of narrative preaching is the certainty that it will be heard. All ears prick up when the advent of a story is announced. Just say, "Once upon a time," and watch your hearers' anticipation play across their faces and surface in their eager movement toward you. If the first aim of preaching is to be heard, then a narrative, almost inevitably, will gain a hearing. If a second aim of preaching is to involve the hearers, then a narrative wins high marks on this score as well. Nearly every textbook that discusses narrative preaching and its possibilities for participation and involvement reminds the readers that Nathan's story of the little ewe lamb, delivered to David after his adultery with Bathsheba and the murder of her husband, is nothing other than an inductive narrative sermon (II Sam. 12:1-7). The sinful king is ensnared in the story immediately, which was the preacher's intent.

A third possibility of narrative preaching is that narrative sermons offer an indirect mode of communication, which may have a greater chance of being heard than a direct mode. In *Overhearing the Gospel*, Craddock says that he has learned from Sören Kierkegaard that the indirect mode of communication is the most suitable for communicating the gospel. This is because the gospel's basic concern is not the transference of information.

> [Kierkegaard] regarded direct as the mode for transferring information and totally appropriate to the fields of history, science, and related disciplines. The indirect is the mode for eliciting capability and action from within the listener, a transaction that does not occur by giving the hearer some information.[19]

Rather than say to David, "All right, you monster! You are a sinner and deserve the hottest spot in Hell," Nathan caught David with his defenses down and his ears eager for a story. Before David knew what had hit him, the dour prophet had him—or rather the evil king had himself. Such is the cleverness of the indirection of the story.

Because narrative sermons are an indirect mode of communication, they are also open-ended. This open-ended nature of the narrative sermon is a fourth possibility of narrative preaching. Narrative sermons provide real opportunities for the hearers to supply their own conclusions to the sermon. This opportunity gives the narrative sermon several advantages over the traditional sermon that tells the hearers what it is they are to conclude.

First, "my" (the hearer's) involvement in the sermon increases when the sermon is open-ended. I am invited into the sermon, coaxed into my response, and urged to think for myself. A narrative sermon positively insists that *I* conclude the sermon, if it is to have any meaning for me personally. Second, I tend to remember and to be moved more deeply by ideas and themes that I have discovered for myself. Until I take an idea and internalize it, it cannot truly be mine. When I do make the idea my own, I give it my own flavor—my own special meaning—and in that process it really does become mine, not just a rehearsal of someone else's thinking; and because it is mine, I will remember it far longer than if I merely had memorized it from another source. Finally, open-endedness in preaching provides openings for the unique work of the Holy Spirit. Our need to control our worship experiences through right timing, clear directions, and printed bulletins can be stifling to the spontaneity of divine worship. This does not mean that any of these "devices" should be abandoned; the order in worship can be an important aid to our encounter with God. Still, because spontaneity is often in short supply, an open-ended sermon may be a great blessing and may provoke an occasion for the activity of the Spirit.

Although open-endedness is a wonderful possibility of narrative preaching, it also can be one of its perils. As Richard Jensen admits, many people are concerned that the hearers of an open-ended sermon will "miss the point."

> But what if we tell a radically open-ended story [a story with no explanation, a pure narrative sermon] and they don't get the point? Or suppose they get the wrong point? Those are the questions most often asked me about story preaching. My response to these kinds of questions is to ask a counter question. "Are you sure they get the point of your conventional sermons?" [20]

Jensen is correct: A preacher can never assume that the hearers get the point of a sermon, no matter what the shape of the sermon may be or how clearly it may be stated. *Every* preacher has had the disconcerting experience of talking to a parishioner about a recently preached sermon and feeling as if two different addresses are the subject of the conversation—the one the preacher preached, and the one the hearer heard! Yet the reason for offering a narrative sermon is not solely to help the hearers get the point. A narrative sermon is preached to engage the congregation, to involve them, and to invite them into the wonder of the gospel. It is my hope that *all* preaching tries to do these things as well, but it is my contention that narrative preaching, when done effectively, has a higher probability of performing these tasks than the "conventional" sermon.

Another peril of narrative preaching is the potential danger of using the biblical stories as artistic ends in themselves. In an article warning against "The Limits of Story,"[21] Richard Lischer first warns against what he calls "aestheticism." According to Lischer, those who fall into this trap "bracket the historical and dogmatic quest in favor of the transient experience of grace."[22] The texts are torn from their roots and are isolated as examples of general experience, thereby losing the sting of their particularity. This criticism is clearly leveled at the "new" literary critics, who give no consideration to the circumstances of the writing of a narrative, but attempt to concentrate on the narrative itself. In chapter 3, I will illustrate that a narrative reading does not depend on the denial of the historical context; the historical context is very important for a full understanding of the narrative. Thus Lischer's critique is aimed at a small group of critics who have fallen out of the mainstream of literary criticism and biblical literary criticism.

Continuing his discussion of the threat of aestheticism, Lischer claims that a preacher becomes a narrator and, thus, one of the story's actors when he or she tells a story. In so doing, the preacher further distances himself or herself from those in the pews. This critique is weak on two grounds. First, the narrator of a story is not automatically an actor in the story. As we have seen, the narrators of the Bible are *narrators,* not actors. Second, a story does not distance a person from the hearers; on the contrary, a story is designed to bridge distances, to offer an indirect mode of communication that involves the hearers in the narrative so that they may see themselves in the story. Even so, a certain distance is necessary for effective communication. The power of story is that it offers distance of subject while bridging the distance of communicating that subject.

Although I find Lischer less than persuasive in his specific critique of the dangers of aestheticism, it is wise to remember that bad narrative preaching can and does fall into this trap. The story can become so entertaining, so much fun, that the congregation becomes an audience and the sermon a comedic or tragic monologue—an end in itself.

Lischer's article also warns against the "ontological" limits of the story. According to Lischer, "Not everyone *has* stories."[23] He refers to the seriously handicapped, the addicted, the poverty-stricken, as those who may *need* stories, but because they have only "immediate needs" and are bewildered "at the unrelatedness of things," they cannot hear them. By making this critique, Lischer suggests that stories need hearers who have the leisure and the capacity to hear them. But I argue that stories, because of their indirect mode, can break through to persons, *especially* to those who cannot voice their own story. Isn't the gospel a story told on behalf of the voiceless ones of society? Experiences of Bible study in the so-called Third World make that claim a reality. Lischer assumes that stories are "neat packages, rounding life off."[24] Many bad stories are neat and rounded-off, but I am hard-pressed to find many such stories in the biblical tradition.

Lischer's most important warning cautions against "sociopolitical limits":

> The story form seemed to reflect more adequately the tentativeness and uncertainty of the age. If we could not speak with assurance of God and summon our hearers to faith and justice as the *telos* of the Christian life, we could with growing theological warrant reflect with our congregations on the richness and inter-relatedness of experience.[25]

According to Lischer's argument, story can turn us away from others and toward ourselves. Preaching, then, can become a self-indulgent exercise in individualized pleasure. Lischer contends that there is another fallout from this turn inward: "It can be argued that story does not provide the resources for implementing ethical growth or sociopolitical change."[26] These are serious charges and have within them an important warning, but again I argue that these results of narratives are neither inevitable nor necessary. The history of Israel itself is witness to that fact. Israel literally survived on its stories, finding in them the source of both stability and change. For more than three thousand years, Israelites and Jews have found hope and challenge in the telling and retelling of the story of the exodus from Egypt. From that story arose the demand for "ethical growth" and, above all, the impetus for "sociopolitical change." Even so, Lischer is right to warn us against the cheap use of stories for self-massage and comfortable spiritual locker-room pep talks. Using stories to avoid the social implications of the gospel of Christ is misusing them and falsifying the gospel itself. The Bible is a vital and living witness to the fact that stories are far more than entertaining forays into our individualized psyches. The stories of the Bible are packed with power for individual and social change.

A final peril of narrative preaching is that it can become a mere performance. This peril holds a two-sided danger. First, the preacher can forget that the story to be told, whether a biblical or personal story, is merely a "lens" for the Christian story, rather than a dramatic act for the sake of the drama. There remains a fine line between a moving narrative sermon and a potent dramatic show. When I experience a powerful African-American sermon, especially one that includes "chording" or "the whoop," [27] I sometimes wonder if the preacher is performing rather than preaching. But what makes this kind of sermon *preaching*, rather than performing, is the context in which it is done. The dialogue style of African-American worship draws from the preacher all the dramatic power that he or she can muster. Nevertheless, what is preaching in that liturgical context may be performance in another context.

The second danger of this peril of "performance" is that the preacher may not have the creativity necessary for the effective use of the story. Ronald Sleeth has said,

> A final caution as to the use of story comes at the point of aesthetics. . . . Many [cultural manifestations—literature, theater, music] assume a creative bent and training many preachers do not have. It could be possible that it is more difficult for a working pastor to master aesthetics than dogmatics or exegesis.[28]

This caution needs to be emphasized. In the next chapter I introduce a kind of biblical analysis that requires creativity to perform well. To translate the biblical reading into a sermon requires an imaginative creativity as great as that required to read the biblical text. All preachers have a measure of creativity and a measure of imagination. Whether or not an individual has enough of both to attempt the kind of preaching I am suggesting is a decision only he or she can make. I believe that preachers are more creative and more imaginative than they think and, if given permission, can unleash both in the service of the gospel.[29] The style of preaching I am suggesting is tailored so that the forces of creativity and imagination can "slip their leash." Still, the decision to unleash these forces is left to the individual.

READING THE BIBLE'S NARRATIVE

A REVOLUTION IN BIBLICAL STUDIES

Not only is there a revolution in the field of preaching, but there is also a revolution in the field of biblical studies. A revolution is two distinct yet related activities: change—the overthrow of an established order or system of thought; and revolution—a cycle or turning around a center. First let us explore how this revolution in the field of biblical studies has involved change.

When Walter Wink made his much-quoted and much-maligned claim that "historical biblical criticism is bankrupt," he fired the opening shots of an intellectual revolution.[1] In *The Bible in Human Transformation,* he says,

> A business which goes bankrupt is not valueless, nor incapable of producing useful products. It still has an inventory of expensive parts, a large capital outlay, a team of trained personnel, a certain reputation, and usually, until the day bankruptcy is declared, a facade which appeared to most to be relatively healthy.[2]

Only one thing is wrong with the business Wink describes: It has ceased to do the thing that is its avowed purpose—it has stopped making money. Therefore, it must declare bankruptcy. For Wink, the historical-critical method of biblical study, a method that has ruled the discipline for more than one hundred years, has become "incapable of achieving what most of its practitioners considered its purpose to be."[3] That purpose is "so to interpret the

Scriptures that the past becomes alive and illuminates our present with new possibilities for personal and social transformation." [4]

Although I sympathize with Wink's desire to find in the biblical text "new possibilities for personal and social transformation," his accusation that the historical-critical method has failed to fulfill this desire is both an overstatement and a misstatement. It is an overstatement because the goals of the historical-critical method are not as broad and "world changing" as Wink assumes them to be. The "central concern" of the historical-critical method is the attempt "to find the meaning of the biblical text by locating its author."[5] *Author* here can mean *creator, teller,* as well as *writer.* The historical critic's work began when "observable discrepancies" within biblical narratives became obvious to the critics. The source critic, the historical critic most concerned with the origins of the material at hand, reconstructs the raw materials of the given text based on the assumption that the discovered sources, as newly reconstructed, would be readable as a text that conforms to recognizable criteria for readable texts. For example, if the source critic assumes that writers do not write repetitive texts (see Gen. 12, 20, 26), then it follows that the repetitions are signs of multiple authorship.

Next, the form critic probes more deeply into the text in an attempt to discover an even older "author" of the materials that make up the text. If the source critic wishes to discover the author of a source (e.g., J, E, D), then the form critic searches for the author of the material that makes up the sources—smaller units that once had independent life but now form part of the building blocks of the source. These blocks often are thought to be oral in origin. Not only is the form critic looking for the "author" of the unit, but she or he is also suggesting that the unit is a way to reconstruct the social life and institutions of ancient Israel and early Christianity. Hence, both form critics and source critics are searching for their respective "authors," a search that arose from an "overwhelming desire to understand, to perceive the text as intelligible—a desire frustrated unless the text is cut into pieces."[6]

With this understanding of the historical-critical method, we can see that Wink's implication that this method did not create the context wherein "the past becomes alive" is in error. Indeed, making the past come alive was precisely the goal of the method, because the search for the various authors was a search for the reasons for their writing, and for the specific things they wanted to say to their ancient audiences. Furthermore, when *rightly applied*, the historical-critical method does not stop with a search for ancient sources and the building blocks of those sources. Instead, the critic moves back toward the text's present unity by searching for the author or authors who assembled the blocks into sources. The critic asks, "How did the formal units get put together in such a way as to create the sources?" This is the work of *redaction criticism.* Redaction criticism assumes that I can comprehend the source fully only when I comprehend the various ways in which the author used, shaped, and ordered the units of material that compose the source I have identified. Klaus Koch calls redaction criticism the "last form-critical process," wherein "a written text is interpreted against the background of its literary type, setting in life, and its transmission history." [7] In other words, the text comes back together again, and the historical critic asks why the text has this kind of unity, as opposed to any other kind.

Redaction criticism arose because the success of the form and source critics suggested that the final form of the biblical text was a "shambles of inconsistency and meandering narrative thread," and those who left it in this mess were little better than "hacks." [8] However, as the critics perceived larger unities and conscious artistry, they took a second look at those "hacks." One example of a second look was Gerhard Von Rad's commentary on Genesis. He argued that a redactor purposely united Genesis 10 to primeval history (Gen. 1–11) to create a new theological whole, thereby witnessing to a God who is both creator and sustainer of the universe.[9]

Thus, in Wink's own words, he would have to admit that Von Rad's work—so richly informed by source, form, and redaction criticism—"illuminates our present with new possibilities for personal and social transformation." Wink has thus contradicted his own accusation against the historical-critical method. Historical-critical methodology is designed to do exactly what Wink says it has not done, and what, in fact, it *has* done when rightly and artfully applied.

Nevertheless, we must not consign Wink's criticism to the dustbin too readily. As is often the case in revolutionary rhetoric, the position is dramatically overstated. However, such rhetoric touches a deep core of dissatisfaction with the fields of biblical studies as they have been practiced and taught. It is true that the most difficult task my students have is harnessing the historical-critical methodology to the new yoke of the sermon. The movement from text to sermon, a problem that has been the source of so much homiletical ink, is very difficult for many. My colleagues in the biblical disciplines often have agreed that the problem lies in the inability or unwillingness of students to appropriate the rich gains of the historical-critical method in ways to make their preaching (or teaching, or counseling) fully informed biblically. No seminary faculty member would deny this lament—nor would very many students, if they were found in a confessing mood. Still, what is troubling is the decisive gap that sometimes is created by a poor application of the historical-critical methodology between "way back then" and "now." Why do my preaching students, and many of the sermons I hear both in and out of the seminary classroom, either drag the Bible kicking and screaming into the twentieth century—with thirty centuries of mud still clinging to its winding sheets—or throw a barely audible nod in the Bible's direction as they careen headlong toward the "relevant," basically unscriptural word?

This question leads us to the second "activity" in the biblical studies revolution: revolving. Revolutions do not always lead to the complete destruction of the system against which they are in revolt. A revolution, after all, is a cycle, a turning around a center. Revolutions against systems are fueled by the conviction that the revolutionaries are more capable than the establishment of performing the crucial tasks needed for the proper functioning of the society in question. And the revolutionaries are more than willing to use any and all tools, even those used by the former wielders of power, to accomplish their revolutionary goals. Wink's economic metaphor helps to illustrate this point.

When a corporation or individual declares bankruptcy, protection from creditors is the primary concern: If the creditors are given a free hand to absorb all cash reserves, then the corporation or individual is effectively wiped out. However, under the protection of chapter 11 of the American Federal Law Code, one can be protected from one's creditors in order to restructure the corporation so that the attainment of profitability once again is possible. Two American corporations, Chrysler and Continental Airlines, have used this legal means with great effectiveness in recent years and are once again viable business entities. The key to the provision is the term *restructuring*. It is my contention that restructuring is presently occurring in biblical studies, especially in terms of method. This fact is evidenced by the veritable flood of volumes that address the questions of methodology either directly or indirectly.

To suggest that restructuring is occurring in biblical studies is not to say that historical-critical study is no longer important. The historical-critical method is neither dead nor dying. No serious reader of the Bible can afford to neglect the crucial findings of this scholarly movement. Indeed, the Bible cannot be read seriously without placing it in its context. To neglect the place, time, and circumstance of the Bible's composition is to tear the material from its life-giving roots. The result of such an uprooting is like that of a careless gardener disturbing the roots of a flowering plant. The flowers wither; then the plant dies. Those who claim to read the Bible with no concern for historical questions are, in effect, handling a dead plant. The biblical methodology discussed in this book takes very seriously the relevant historical background of the texts under consideration. Despite my refutation of Wink's formulation of the problem, I do believe that the historical-critical method of biblical study, as currently practiced, *is* approaching bankruptcy and needs the restructuring that is now beginning. Part of that restructuring will be facilitated by the methodology that has been called literary analysis.

THE NARRATIVE ART OF THE BIBLE

The work of William Shakespeare has been and will continue to be understood and appreciated by different readers on different levels. T. S. Eliot refers to the multilayered genius of Shakespeare in this way:

> For the simplest audience there is the plot, for the more thoughtful the character and the conflict of character, for the more literary the words and phrasing, for the more musically sensitive the rhythm, and for auditors of greater sensitiveness and understanding a meaning which reveals itself gradually.[10]

Most of us who read *Julius Caesar* in high school struggled mightily just to understand the plot of the drama. For some of us, that was achievement enough! But others of us, after reading the play again and again, and seeing the play again and again, reached deeper levels of understanding and appreciation. This was so for at least two important reasons. First, our acquaintance with the language of the playwright—with his plots, his characterizations, his thematic interests—increased commensurate with our contact with this specific play and with other plays in the Shakespeare corpus. Second, we were made to believe that Shakespeare was great literature. We could deepen our analytical skills because we were told, and finally came to see for ourselves, that there are profound depths to plumb. The purpose of exploring the narrative art of the Bible is to illustrate that all that has been said of Shakespeare is true of the Bible as well.

That claim may appear to be so self-evident that it does not merit any discussion whatsoever. It is my conviction, however, that one of the highest hurdles needing to be vaulted in an attempt to evaluate the narrative art of the Bible is the belief that the Bible is primitive literature and therefore is not great art. "Oh, it is a classic all right, and it is, of course, holy; but it was written a very long time ago by persons who were little removed from barbarism." Ironically, this belief is compounded by the kind of biblical scholarship that has been practiced for the past one hundred and fifty years.

Although I have no intention of announcing the demise of the historical-critical method, I suggest that there is another way to approach the narrative texts of the Bible that can bear good fruit for preaching: literary analysis. A shift needs to be made here from "composition as *genesis* to composition as *poesis*."[1] Rather than asking, "Who wrote this?" the reader assumes that the narrator is omniscient; that is, the narrator is privileged to tell the story in any way he or she wants. Rather than asking, "Did this happen like this?" the reader asks, "Why did this narrator write about this character like this?" The reader asks questions such as, "Why was the narrator so assured when he or she described that incident, yet so ambiguous when describing this one?" and "What does the narrator mean when he or she has the character say this instead of that?" and "Why does the character repeat the command word-for-word here, but alter the command slightly there?" These are the questions of poesis, or literary analysis. I use the term *analysis* rather than *criticism* because the discipline of *literary criticism* in some quarters of the biblical guild is identical to *source criticism*. What I mean by the term *literary analysis* is the polar opposite of *literary criticism* when defined as the search for sources.

Before discussing literary analysis in detail, we must address an important question: Is this sort of approach appropriate for the Bible, which is first and foremost a sacred book and, in that regard, is wholly unlike any other book? Many critics argue that literary analysis is not an appropriate approach. James Kugel, for example, warns that one should be deeply suspicious of reading the Bible in this way:

> What is literary about the Bible at all? Certainly it does not identify itself as literature, and often such [God-oriented] self-definition as does occur seems clearly to . . . suppose a relationship between speaker and hearer which, we somehow feel, is double-crossed by being looked at *as* literature, as artful composition, as anything more than a faithful and naive recording.[12] ← *all it is?*

The implication of his use of the word *faithful* is that a literary reading and a faithful reading are potentially incompatible. Whereas Kugel warns of the dangers of an application of literary canons to the biblical text, Kenneth Gros Louis urges, on the contrary, that such an application must be done *only* without any interest in what the author had in mind or without any concern for the religious implications of the writing.[13]

In response to Kugel's warning, I offer these observations. The Bible's narrators chose to express their thoughts in the mode of narrative. It is therefore incumbent upon us to examine that narration if we are to gain access to the narrator's concerns. Because the narratives *are* narratives, no more and no less, they must be examined for their artfulness. If we fail to do this, then we make the assumption that the writing is no more than a "faithful and naive recording." Such language lands us perilously close to a view of the Bible as a kind of divine automatic writing, a view that tends to remove it from any sort of analysis at all.

Gros Louis, on the other hand, has made the common mistake of failing to distinguish between the "meaning" of a written piece, which does not change, and its "significance," which changes nearly as often as it is read.[14] Unless the interpreter can gain at least limited access to authorial intention (here one finds the chief gains of the historical-critical method, when rightly applied), no interpretations can be judged valid or invalid. Every interpreter knows that there are interpretations that are in some sense "better" than other interpretations. For example, how can I say that the odious "eternal black slavery curse," which was read in a combination of Genesis 9 and 10 for many years in England and America is not a valid reading? Unless I can say that the *meaning* of the passage clearly will not allow such a reading to be valid, then certain racist groups could claim the authority of the Bible for their exclusivist claims. But I can reject such a reading because the *meaning* of the passage, which in part is the passage's intention, will not allow that particular *significance* to be judged valid.

A literary analysis of the Bible's narratives is not only compatible with the Bible's faith claims, but also is essential to the achievement of a clearer discernment of those claims. Furthermore, a literary analysis of the Bible's narratives is not incommensurate with the concerns of the historical-critical method. In fact, both are needed to interpret fully the riches of the narratives of the Bible. Thus, to understand the narratives of the Hebrew Bible in their fullness, we must employ the techniques of literary analysis. If we are not aware of these techniques, then we cannot appropriate the riches of the narrative—that is, we will not be able to discern how the narratives accomplish the tasks that the narrators set out for them to perform. And if we are not able to hear the texts in their fullness, then we will not be able to create textually based narrative sermons that attempt to bring to contemporary hearers the power and vitality that are the result of the detailed techniques of those narrators.

To hear these narratives anew, we must first retrain our eyes and ears. Let us focus our attention on three broad categories of narrative techniques in order to begin this retraining: plot, character and characterization, and point of view. Although these techniques may at first appear quite foreign to you, they enable us to uncover the means by which the ancient narrators presented their stories and made those stories vibrantly unforgettable. From these techniques we may learn how *our* narrative sermons can achieve the same vitality and memorability.

Narrative
plot, character, characterization,
pt. of view

Plot

Plot can be defined as the dynamic, sequential element in narrative literature. Insofar as character, or any other element in narrative, becomes dynamic, it is a part of the plot.[15]

Most narratives, and certainly all biblical narratives, may be characterized by a *dynamic, sequential element.* These two adjectives are significant. To have a plot, a narrative must be *dynamic*—that is, characterized by action. More specifically, whereas *story* is a general term for character and action in a narrative form, *plot* is intended to reflect "action alone, with the minimum possible reference to character."[16] Plot also must be *sequential.* If art presents its materials simultaneously or randomly, there is no plot.

Although T. S. Eliot rather condescendingly relegates plot to the "simplest of audiences"—implying that to look only for plot is to miss the deeper riches of narrative—plot is central to the appropriation of all narrative. This is so because of the expectations that all readers bring to narrative. The most common expectation is that of cause and effect. In *Rhetoric of Fiction,* Wayne Booth says, "Not only do we believe that certain causes do in life produce certain effects; in literature we believe that they should."[17]

The cycle of Jacob stories in Genesis 25–50 is an example of the expectation of cause and effect. First we observe the wily Jacob trick Esau and then Laban. Upon his return to Israel, after his confrontation with the mysterious "man" at the Jabbok river (32:22-32) and his tearful meeting with a surprisingly forgiving Esau, we expect Jacob to drop his trickster modus vivendi and join his brother in a new-found harmony. After all, he has just announced that to see Esau is to "see the face of God" (33:10). But we are surprised to hear that though Jacob promises to follow Esau to Seir (33:14), he in fact journeys alone to Succoth (33:17), adding this small lie to the many he has told before.

Our expectations for the consequences of lying behavior are not satisfied by the end of chapter 33, but the story has not ended. In the subsequent account of the rise of Joseph, Jacob is cruelly lied to and tricked by his own sons—not the least of whom is Joseph, his favorite. Joseph's cruel game of cat and mouse with his brothers inevitably leads to Jacob's heart-rending decision to relinquish his new favorite, Benjamin, into the less-than-trustworthy hands of his sons—who themselves plotted the demise of Joseph so long before. When Jacob says, "You will bring down my gray hairs with sorrow to Sheol" (Gen. 42:38), the reader achieves the satisfaction that Jacob's earlier behavior has had its consequences after all.[18]

The story of David is another example of cause and effect. David was the golden one who seemed always to land on his feet. Time after time he was saved from his own reckless ambitions in very unlikely ways. When it appeared that he would be forced to fight on the side of the Philistines against his own people, David was rescued at the last moment by the Philistines themselves (I Sam. 29). When his anger got the better of him and he determined to kill the churlish Nabal for slighting him, he was rescued from the deed by Nabal's own wife, Abigail (I Sam. 25). The plot of the story cries out for redress for David's often immoral behavior. Eventually it comes. After David's affair with Bathsheba and his murder of her husband, Uriah, one of his sons rapes one of his daughters and is in turn killed by another son. That son later usurps his father's throne and is killed, against David's express command, by Joab. These appalling tragedies lead to a final scene in which the old, pathetic David is trembling in his bed, unable to stay warm despite the attentions of the beautiful Abishag. As the stories of David and Jacob illustrate, cause leads inexorably to effect. In the Bible's narratives, the dynamic sequence of plot provides an important window into the art of the narrator.

Character and Characterization

Actions and Speech

> What is character but the determination of incident? What is incident but the illustration of character? What is either a picture or a novel that is *not* of character? What else do we seek in it and find in it? It is an incident for a woman to stand up with her hand resting on a table and look out at you in a certain way; or if it be not an incident I think it will be hard to say what it is.[19]

Although Henry James's claim that character and incident (event or action) are inextricably bound together was based on his reading of nineteenth-century novels, he summarizes well one

of the important ways in which biblical narrators delineate character. We gain insight into the Bible's characters primarily by
observing what they *do*. Although the narrator does not tell us
directly what sort of man Saul is when he first introduces him in
I Samuel 9, we can observe his actions and thereby be led to discover characteristics of this man who is to be the first king of
Israel. Saul dutifully searches for the lost donkeys of his father,
but when they cannot be found he urges a return home empty-
handed. It is his unnamed servant who insists that they push on,
who suggests that they visit the mysterious seer to aid the search,
and who produces the money to pay the man. All these actions
appear to suggest that Saul is an ill-prepared, hesitant, and cau-
tious man. When Saul is found hiding among the bags on his public
coronation day and has to be dragged up to the dais to receive the
crown (I Sam. 10), the reader is probably not altogether surprised.

To fully understand and appreciate the actions of characters, it
is helpful to recognize a character's function or purpose in the
story. According to Adele Berlin, all characters may be described
as either *round* or *flat*. Saul is an example of a round character—a
character who is fully drawn and richly portrayed.[20] The opposite
of the round character is the flat character—a character who
functions merely as an agent in the story. The Amalekite king,
Agag, is a flat character. In I Samuel 15, Agag appears as merely a
sign of Saul's incomplete destruction of the Amalekites. Later he
functions as the object of Samuel's demonstration to Saul just
how he should have treated the vanquished king (I Sam. 15:33).
Although Agag displays one emotion and utters one line, he
remains only a flat functionary.

Berlin offers some helpful distinctions among those characters
she calls agents. Agents appear on a continuum that moves from
those about whom little is known (e.g., Agag) to those about
whom much is known. However, even though we may know a
good deal about a character, that character still may be only a
functionary or what Berlin calls an "exaggerated stereotype."[21] She
lists Abigail and her husband Nabal in this category (I Sam. 25). It
is accurate to consign Nabal to the role of stereotype. His name
means "fool," a fact announced by the narrator in verse 3, and by
his own wife as she tries to defend him before an enraged David
in verse 25. He is a churlish, drunken brute, and no reader is

grieved when the Lord strikes him dead. However, I am not convinced that Abigail is merely a stereotype. She certainly is the "beautiful and clever damsel to the rescue," a character beloved by many writers, but her lengthy speech to David, which covers nearly ten verses of the text—an extraordinarily long speech in the Hebrew Bible—is a masterpiece of subtle rhetoric that is designed to cool off the infuriated David, to massage his ever-demanding ego, and to ingratiate herself into his favor. In my opinion, this speech elevates Abigail above the level of a stock character and brings her closer to a "full-fledged" character. Berlin finds the speech to be "out of all proportion at the end of the story when David proposes marriage."[22] But that is just the point! Abigail's brilliant speech has made all this possible.

In biblical narrative, what characters *say*—or do not say—is as important as what they *do*. In Genesis 12:10-20, the character of Abram is placed in a very compromising light both in his actions and in his speeches. When he and his wife are traveling to Egypt to escape a famine, Abram appears to have only one thing on his mind. In a three-verse speech to a silent Sarai, Abram urges her to lie about their relationship, "in order that it may go well with me because of you, and that my life may be spared on your account" (vs. 13). Abram wants to be safe and rich, and he plans to sacrifice his wife to obtain both of these things. Things happen as Abram had hoped until God intrudes to save the abandoned wife and to throw a serious crimp into Abram's plan for a comfortable retirement in Egypt. When pharaoh confronts Abram with his lying deed, Abram astonishingly says nothing at all; the voluble Abram of a few verses ago is now strangely silent. He simply leaves "with his wife and all that he had." Thus, both Abram's actions and his words—or lack of words—raise several red flags for the reader.

The characterization of pharaoh in Exodus 1:8-22 is a good example of how characterization is accomplished through both deed and speech. A new king comes to the throne of Egypt having no knowledge of Joseph, the wise Hebrew who saved Egypt from the terrible famine and who was the confidant of a previous pharaoh. Not only does he not know of Joseph, but he also regards Joseph's descendants as a problem. He says that they are "too many and too strong for us." So the pharaoh institutes what

what would he say about God a biography?

appears to be a wise plan. His plan is to work the Israelites nearly to death so that the last thing on their minds when they return home from the brick quarries each night is procreation. Pharaoh gives the orders calmly and forcefully, because at this point he is in control of the situation. But the plan does not work. In fact, it appears to have the opposite effect. "The more they were oppressed, the more they multiplied and the more they spread abroad." Now the wise pharaoh and his people are in dread of the Israelites, and his control begins to slip.

So the pharaoh formulates another plan. He calls two midwives to the throne room and instructs them to kill all male children when assisting in the births of Israelites. However, they are instructed to allow all female babies to live. In this the king of Egypt shows himself to be less than wise in speech and deed. Perhaps a wiser plan would have been to kill the females. Nevertheless, the midwives flatly refuse to obey his direct orders. In a rage, the pharaoh summons them to his chambers and asks, "Why have you done this thing? You have let the boy babies live!" The midwives respond calmly, "Not like Egyptian women are these Hebrew women. They are full of life! Before the midwives can reach them, they have already delivered!" The answer to pharaoh's question is that the Israelites possess an abundance of life. Surely the midwives' response is exaggerated, for not *all* Hebrew women are able to deliver without help. Nevertheless, they say it is so and pharaoh believes them.

In response to this insulting and incredible reply, pharaoh *commands* the women to act. However, by this time his authority is minimal at best, and his mind is not what it once was. "So pharaoh commanded all his people, 'Every son that is born, you shall throw into the Nile, but let every daughter live!' " All of pharaoh's own people are now commanded to kill *all* male babies by tossing them into the Nile, but to allow every daughter to live. Is the pharaoh so terribly shaken by the frustration of his plans that he will stop at nothing to destroy the Israelites, even to the horrible absurdity of sacrificing his own male babies?[23] The story seems to support this conclusion. Egyptian sons *are* sacrificed, and Hebrew babies are thrown into the Nile, or at least one baby in particular is so thrown. But because pharaoh commanded that daughters were to be allowed to live, the daughter of that Hebrew baby's parents conspires with the daughter of pharaoh himself to rescue the child from the Nile who one day saves the people whom pharaoh could not control.

This story illustrates how the characterization of pharaoh is accomplished through his actions and words. Pharaoh first *says,* then *calls,* and finally *commands.* But this verbal intensification is negated by the content of the speeches. Pharaoh plans wisely; then he plots a foolish individual genocide, and finally he madly demands a universal drowning—the only known "victim" of which grows up in his own house and becomes the source of his undoing. Thus, the characterization of pharaoh holds the seeds of his destruction and the destruction of his people.

An analysis of texts such as this one can be achieved by a careful examination of a competent English translation of the Bible. In such an examination, the reader must pay careful attention to the speeches and actions of the characters—actions best seen by the verbs used to describe them. Speeches and especially the verbs used in them are the "stuff" of biblical characterization. It is helpful to underline all speeches of a character with one color of ink and all the verbs connected to that character in another color. In that way, one can see graphically just what the narrator is saying about this character and begin to think about how to present that character in a narrative sermon.

Although the most prominent means of characterization are actions and speeches, another way that biblical narrators delineate their characters is through physical description.

Physical description

It is often noted how few physical descriptions are found in the Bible. In fact, such descriptions are so rare that they are often memorable. Anyone who is familiar with the story of Saul knows that Saul, the first king of Israel, was inordinately tall (I Sam. 9:2; 10:23). Saul also is twice called "handsome" at the very beginning of the story (I Sam. 9:2). These two adjectives are the only physical portraits the narrator shares with us. They are so vague that they lull the reader into passing over them too quickly. However, Saul's height is used in a fascinating and horrifying way in this story. The second time that Saul is called tall is right after he has been found hiding among the baggage on his public coronation day. The incongruity of the tallest man in the land trying to hide among baggage is a warning note to the reader. Then after Saul has committed suicide, he is *beheaded* by the Philistines. The narrator says, literally, "From the shoulders upward he was taller," but his decapitation by the enemy has removed the thing that set him apart from the people. In death, whatever distinctiveness Saul possessed is removed. He was just one of the people after all. This example illustrates that even seemingly insignificant notes of physical description should be taken with seriousness.

Robert Alter offers another example.[24] When David is introduced to us in I Samuel 16:12, he is described in three ways. The narrator tells us that he is ruddy (red-haired), that he has beautiful eyes, and that he is good looking. In the next chapter when David goes out to fight the giant Goliath, these descriptions recur with a thoroughly altered tone. When the giant first catches sight of the tiny David, he scorns him because he is "ruddy with beautiful eyes" (I Sam. 17:42). To Goliath, David is "a red-haired pretty boy with beautiful eyes." That Goliath has woefully misjudged his opponent becomes all too clear when he finds himself face-down in the mud—about to be beheaded by the pretty boy. In an astonishingly detailed description, Goliath is set up for the fall, although generations of readers have seen him as an invincible foe. In I Samuel 17:4-7, we are told of Goliath's enormous height, of his armor and its immense weight, the heavy javelin he carries, and of the impossibly large shaft and head of his spear. Goliath is a figure who strikes terror into the hearts of the Israelites. But to the lithe and able sling-shot artist, Goliath is little more than a tank without an engine.

Note how aptly I Samuel 17:48 describes the so-called battle. "Thus, when the Philistine got up, and went out and drew near to meet David, David rushed quickly toward the line of battle to meet the Philistine." I have translated more literally to make note of the sharp difference in the movements of the antagonists. Goliath, encumbered by his massive size and imposing armor, "gets up, goes out and draws near"—three verbs that offer a picture of ponderous activity. David, on the other hand, "rushes quickly *toward* the line of battle," being careful to stay far away from his nearly immovable foe. If the characterizations are read aright, the battle's outcome is a foregone conclusion. Alter nicely summarizes the scene and offers the ideological power of the narration as well:

> The thematic purpose of this exceptional attention to physical detail is obvious: Goliath moves into the action as a man of iron and bronze, an almost grotesquely quantitative embodiment of a hero, and this hulking monument to an obtusely mechanical conception of what constitutes power is marked to be felled by a clever shepherd boy with his slingshot.[25]

Thus, ideology is clothed in physical detail, and only a careful narrative reading can reveal the subtleties that make the story live and work.

Inner lives of characters

Often critics assert that Hebrew narrative style precludes any serious attention to the inner life of a character. In their book *The Nature of Narrative*, Robert Scholes and Robert Kellogg make this claim:

> The inward life is assumed but not presented in primitive narrative literature, whether Hebraic or Hellenic. This inscrutability of characters, their opaqueness, is neither a defect or a limitation. It is simply a characteristic.[26]

This judgment can be affirmed, however, in only a very restricted sense. The authors cite the example of David to demonstrate their claim. Although it is quite true that one finds very few overt references to the inner thoughts of characters in the story of David, the Bible is not devoid of such statements. In Genesis 37:4, we hear of the hatred that consumes the brothers of Joseph and even are told the reason for this hatred. Later the narrator invites us into the mind of Joseph—now the governor of Egypt—as he confronts his brothers who have come to buy food from him. "Joseph saw his brothers and knew them . . . but they did not know him. And Joseph remembered the dreams which he had dreamed of them" (Gen. 39:7-9). Note the rich portrayal of Joseph's inner life. He sees his brothers, recognizes them, realizes instantly that they do not recognize him, remembers the dreams he dreamt so long ago, and accuses the poor pilgrims of espionage!

70

Other examples of "the inward lives" of biblical characters abound in the Hebrew Bible. In more than a few places the narrator uses the phrase "said in his heart," which means "said to himself." Esau, for example, having just been tricked out of his birthright by the wily Jacob and his equally wily mother, Rebekah, "said in his heart, 'The days of mourning for my father are approaching; then I will kill my brother Jacob'" (Gen. 27:41). This internal monologue, which suggests the rage and frustration Esau feels as he broods over the impending death of the foolish old man who unwittingly has done him in, carries considerable dramatic power. Even God is portrayed as possessing a rich inner life. In Genesis 8:21, after gratefully accepting the pleasing odor of Noah's sacrifice, God speaks in the divine heart and says, "I will never again curse the ground because of the human beings, because the imagination of their hearts is evil from their youth." The very reason for the coming of the flood was the "evil imaginations of the human beings" (Gen. 6:5). Because of that evil, "God was grieved to the divine heart" (v. 6). So it is through the internal monologues of God that the reader is permitted to witness a change in God's heart in relationship to the human creation. We witness the changing heart of God by eavesdropping on the silent thoughts of God.

Contrasting characters

Adele Berlin suggests that another way biblical narrators offer characterizations in their stories is through the technique of three different types of contrast.[27] First, characters may be contrasted with other characters. We already have seen the detailed contrast between David and Goliath. Another example is the contrast between David and Joab in their respective treatment of the rebel Absalom. Whereas David urges that Absalom's life be spared, Joab takes the first opportunity to assault the boy and then allows his soldiers to murder him. After Absalom's death, David is inconsolable while Joab upbraids his king for being weak in the face of the obvious rebellion and for desiring the death of the wrong people. These sharply contrasting portraits tell us much about the characters of David and Joab (see II Sam. 18-19 for the complete story).

A second kind of contrast is the contrast of a character's own actions. One example is the obvious contrast between the two

God's character, esp.

What's been a reality that is inconsistent?

speeches of Judah in Genesis 37:26-27 and 44:18-34. In the former speech, Judah sounds very much like an entrepreneur "on the make," and the product he hopes to peddle is the helpless Joseph. Judah says to his brothers, "What is the profit when we kill our brother and hide his blood? Come now, let's sell him to the Ishmaelites, so that our hands will not be on him. He is after all our brother, our own flesh." This speech is laced with greed, callousness, and bitter sarcasm. But the Judah of the second speech has no greed, callousness, or sarcasm left. In a heartfelt address, Judah tells the awesome and mysterious governor of Egypt—Joseph in disguise—that he will offer his own life for his brothers and his grieving father. Judah pleads, "Let your servant remain instead of the lad [Benjamin] as a slave to my lord." The speech is so moving that in the very next scene Joseph ends his elaborate charade and reveals his true identity to his astonished brothers. Something has happened to the Judah of chapter 37 to be sure.

A third way to characterize through contrast is to describe a character's action in such a way as to call into question the reader's expectations for that character. This technique is related closely to the previous technique, but the difference lies in the realm of surprise or shock. Once again the character of Esau serves as an example. When Jacob finally plans to return to Israel after twenty years of refuge in Haran, he does not expect Esau to have forgotten the terrible wrong that was done to him or his desire to see Jacob dead. When Jacob tries to buy his brother's good favor with a huge and varied bribe (Gen. 32:13-20), the messenger returns with terrifying news: "We came to your brother Esau, and he is coming to meet you, and four hundred men are with him." The end of Jacob the trickster seems to be at hand. But the narrative holds a surprise for Jacob and the reader. When Jacob approaches Esau's assembly, Esau runs to meet him, kisses him, and they weep. Nothing in the narrative has prepared the reader for this event. Esau weeps for joy; Jacob weeps in relief. Perhaps Jacob speaks more truth than he realizes when he says, "Truly, to see your face is like seeing the face of God, with such favor have you received me" (Gen. 33:10). The reader's expectations have been dashed. To see the face of God in Esau's face is truly a surprise.

READING THE BIBLE'S NARRATIVE

Point of View

The third and final narrative technique we will explore is point of view. The recognition of point of view in narrative is at the same time quite simple and infinitely complex. As Robert Scholes and Robert Kellog point out, narrative offers several points of view in its construction.

> In the relationship between the teller and the tale, and that other relationship between the teller and the audience, lies the essence of narrative art. The narrative situation is thus ineluctably ironical. The quality of irony is built into the narrative form as it is into no other form of literature. . . . In any example of narrative art there are, broadly speaking, three points of view—those of the characters, the narrator, and the audience.[28]

Sometimes we see the story through the eyes of one or more characters, and sometimes we see the story through the eyes of an unnamed narrator. Sometimes the point of view can even be the audience of the narrative, or the reader. As Scholes and Kellog explain, it is this complexity of point of view that provides the real pleasure of narrative art.

> We can hazard the notion that stories appeal primarily because they offer a simulacrum of life which enables an audience to participate in events without being involved in the consequences which events in the actual world inevitably carry with them. Our pleasure in narrative literature itself, then, can be seen as a function of disparity of viewpoint or irony.[29]

The narrative artist controls the reader's relationship to the story by the way he or she handles the sources of the story's telling. Thus, the reader's pleasure arises from insight into the disparity between his or her knowledge of the story as reader and the knowledge, or lack of knowledge, demonstrated by various characters in the story. An example from the book of Job illustrates this well.

In the prologue to Job, we see both levels of the drama unfold. We see Job as a righteous man who loses everything in a tragic series of events. We also witness the mysterious scene in heaven

Job— dramatic irony

between God and the satan, which in some way has triggered Job's choice for the test. When the friends of Job arrive on the scene, they do not possess the knowledge that we have been given; they see only the miserable Job and consequently make certain dogmatic conclusions based on their previously held theological positions. We, the readers, know these positions to be cruelly wrong; Job is not on the ash heap of his life because of some sin. The irony is compounded by what Job knows. He knows himself to be innocent of anything worthy of ash heaps, but he knows nothing of the heavenly wager. Thanks to the narrator, we, the readers, know all, but Job knows only his own experience, and Job's friends know nothing of Job's circumstances. The narrator has placed the reader in the pleasurable position of being able to make judgments about the correctness of the positions in the ongoing debate. This is a classic example of what is called *dramatic irony.* The reader is "in the know" while the characters must flounder around in search of whatever knowledge they can discern.

The two reports of the death of Samuel found in I Samuel 31 and II Samuel 1 also exemplify the importance of point of view in assessing the narrator's art. As Adele Berlin notes, nineteenth century historical critics generally solved the "problem" of these two conflicting reports of the death of Saul by assigning the two reports to two different literary sources.[30] Although it may be true that these two chapters arise from two different traditions, the fact remains that they have been joined together. What the literary analyst assumes, in contradistinction to the historical critic, is that the text as it stands makes some kind of literary sense. Some attention to point of view may suggest what kind of sense that may be.

First Samuel 31 is a third-person account of the death of Saul. Because I have found no source critics who question the veracity of this account, this narrator is to be trusted. The narrator tells us that Saul asked his armorbearer to kill him, but that the man refused. Saul was forced to take his own life—the ultimate demonstration of his complete isolation. Saul's body is desecrated by the "uncircumcised Philistines" and then rescued for proper burial by the heroic Jabesh-Gileadites.

When confronted by a different account of the tragedy in the next chapter, the reader is appropriately suspicious. If the second account were also a third-person account from the same narrator, the reader would have considerable difficulty deciding which of the tales to trust. However, attention to point of view demonstrates that this is not a problem. The second account is a first-person narration of Saul's death told by an Amalekite—a member of the group of people who were odious in the sight of God for their dastardly attempt to impede the progress of the chosen people as they went forth out of Egypt (I Sam. 15). Before this Amalakite opens his mouth, the reader is prepared by the story and by the narrator's own account not to trust his tale.

The way in which the story is told corroborates the reader's suspicions. The Amalakite appears before David with the look of a mourner. His clothes are appropriately torn and he has sprinkled dirt upon his head. He shows proper deference to David by doing obeisance to him and by waiting to speak until he is spoken to. When David asks from where he has come, the man tells him that he has just arrived from the camp of Israel and that he is, in fact, an escapee from that camp. David urges him to tell his story. The Amalekite tells David about the battle: "The people have fled from the combat, but also many of the people have fallen and died. Even Saul and his son Jonathan are dead." David then asks how he knows this to be true. The Amalekite's reply is perhaps overly creative.

> I happened to find myself on Mt. Gilboa. There was Saul, leaning on his spear; there were the chariots and horsemen standing near him! Then he glanced behind him and saw me. "Who are you?" And I said to him, "An Amalekite am I." And he said to me, "Stay near me and kill me, for anguish [?] has seized me, because all my life remains with me." So I stood near to him and killed him, for I knew that he would not live after he had fallen. Then I took the crown from his head and the armlet from his arm, and I have brought these very things to my lord. (II Sam. 1:6-10, author's translation)

This speech raises several questions. First, how did he just "happen" to be on Mt. Gilboa? Is the man a soldier? He identifies himself to David in verse 13 as the "son of a resident alien;" he gives no indication that he is in Saul's army. Second, the rhetoric of his speech is too detailed. It has the sound of rehearsal rather than the sound of a genuinely mourning man who has just slain a king.

Third, it is too dramatic. Twice in the first line he uses the ejaculatory demonstrative word *hinneh*, which means *behold* or *look*. One can easily picture the sweeping arm gestures and upraised eyebrows that might accompany such a grand speech. Fourth, the speech ends with an ill-disguised plea for favor in the attempt to give the stolen regal insignia to David. But David knew the thieving propensities of Amalekites, having just witnessed their larceny on his own wives and family not many days prior to this scene (see I Sam. 30).

The narrator's art has made it clear that this wandering, opportunistic Amalekite is not to be trusted. He juxtaposes his own clear-eyed account of Saul's death to this self-serving account, in which an Amalekite serves as the first-person witness. With this brilliant use of point of view, the narrator reveals much to the reader.

◆　◆　◆

In chapter 2, I affirmed, with Fred Craddock, that preaching is an attempt to affirm God's way in the world by aligning one's preaching with the "mode and matter" of that way. This chapter has illustrated how the Bible as narrative art is important to this endeavor. In biblical narrative, the form (mode) is inextricably connected to the content (matter). To preach narratively, one must be able to read narratively to maintain this inextricable union of mode and matter.

Can anyone learn the techniques of narrative reading? The answer is yes; anyone can learn to read narratively by doing three things consecutively. First, read with your eyes open for the indications of plot, character, and point of view as exemplified in this chapter. (Reading the text in Hebrew provides additional insights into the subtleties of the text, but those gains are more quantitative than qualitative. Reliable translations will yield many insights to the careful reader.) Second, consult critical commentaries for additional linguistic details. Very few commentaries to date are concerned with questions of poesis, so do not expect much of this nature from them. However, after—and only after—you have done your careful poetic reading, a critical commentary can provide much linguistic detail. Third, consult the growing number of books that use poetics in the analysis of Hebrew narrative (see the bibliography). *Do not* read them before you have a chance to do your own work on the text. This is true for any exegesis, but it is especially important when attempting a narrative exegesis.

Now that we have considered the *what* and the *why* of narrative preaching, we must turn to the *how*. How can we move from a narrative reading of the biblical text to a narrative sermon based on that text? Comments within the narrative sermons in chapters 4 and 5 help to illustrate how this is done by referring to the discussions in chapters 2 and 3.

A PURE NARRATIVE SERMON:
THE BEST LAUGH OF ALL

The old man brought the load of wood closer to the fire. It was dusk, and the air was chill. But the silence was a blessing; it gave the old man time to think. One-hundred-year-old men need time to think; there is so much to think about. He poked his old knife into the coals to stir them to life. His mind wandered back . . . and back. He remembered God's first call as if it were yesterday. Even an old man could never forget the call of the mysterious God. "Abram," God had said—that had been his name until God had changed it—"Go from your country, your friends in Haran, and your own father's household to a land that I will show you." And the old man had done it—just like that. A small grin played across his face as he thought of his hurried departure to this unknown land. Oh, his friends had asked him about it; so had his father. But the old man had simply said, "God has called me." He didn't talk much in those days.

I have tried to do several things in this opening. First, I focus squarely on Abraham, as the beginning, middle, and end of Genesis 22 suggest I should do. It is best not to introduce other characters too soon. Second, I introduce the three objects that will be central to the near-sacrifice later—wood, fire, and knife. Third, I introduce the history of this man, the "these things" of Genesis 22:1, to set the context for God's call to him. Fourth, because God's call has occurred before I must get that in front of my hearers in order to set up the new call that is about to happen. Fifth, I introduce the theme of Abraham's talking or lack of talking, an important element in the story of Abraham. Sixth, I stress Abraham's first obedience. Note also that the increasing difficulty of what he is called to leave—country, friends, family—is brought up to be recalled later in God's request concerning his son. I have tried to use items and thoughts that will play a role later in the sermon. As in the biblical narrative, I have tried to waste few words.

But circumstances made quite a talker out of him later. No sooner had he gotten to the land when a famine hit. "I did what I had to do," he thought. "I know that God had promised that I would become a great nation, that this new land would be the start of it, and that I would be a blessing to the whole world." A tiny chuckle went up from the old man's weathered face. "God knew," he thought, "that my wife couldn't have any kids. But God picked us anyway." The old man had often wondered about the reasons for some of God's decisions; they somehow seemed so absurd! He shook his head a bit to try to get back to his memories. He and Sarai—that was her name before God had changed it—had left for Egypt. There was always food in Egypt. But he had been scared. Well, who wouldn't be? I mean, she was beautiful, and pharaoh was rich and powerful. Why, a fellow could get killed, his wife could be stolen, and his future could be cut off! Of course he had lied! It was a good one, too. The old man laughed out loud when he thought of that clever lie. "Say you're my sister," he had said, "so that it may be well with me because of you, and that my life will be spared on your account." Oh, that was a good one, all right! And those crazy Egyptians had bought the whole thing; they were always gullible. The old man remembered with relish the gold and silver that the pharaoh had showered on him. Well, she was beautiful; she should have brought a good price.

The old man paused. He had thrown the promise of God away when he lied. But he had been scared, and God saved the day anyway. No harm done. And it had been fun to watch those Egyptians suffer from the plague God had given them; how they had howled! And how old pharaoh had screamed at him to take his wife back. It seemed just like yesterday. And they had left, richer and still together. No harm done!

I tell the story of Genesis 12 at some length to establish the character of Abraham and to introduce Sarah. Here Abraham is loquacious and clever—a man not committed to the promise of God but concerned only with himself. This emphasis is to allow the hearers to wonder just how this man will act when the great test begins. Surely the ancient hearers of the story also wondered about the outcome of the test. Abraham is, after all, one of them and one of us. I also continue to reinforce the theme of laughter, since the name Isaac means "laughter"—an idea I will use again in the sermon. I must move on now, lest the early material overpower the text at hand.

A loud pop from the fire broke his silent memory. It was full dark now. The donkeys were still; no sounds came from the tent. Sarah was in there. Ishmael and his mother, Hagar, slept in another tent nearby. The thought of Hagar revived the old man's memory. It was Sarah's idea, after all. She wanted a child; it was terrible for a woman of the tents not to have a child. "She offered Hagar to me," he thought. "Yes, I remember what God had said; the promised child was to be mine and Sarah's. But, heaven knows, I wasn't getting any younger, and Sarah was no blushing damsel either!"

"We will just adopt the child as our own," she had said. Why not? No harm done. The old man remembered his time with the young Egyptian maid with pleasure; they had produced a son. Ishmael, they had called him: "God hears!" Both the old man and Sarah had thought that was that; they had a child, and the mysterious promise of blessing for the whole world was now assured.

But they were wrong. When the old man suggested Ishmael was the child of the promise, God said loudly, "No." God said it would be Sarah's child and nobody else's. When the old man thought of that, he gave a great belly laugh and clapped his old hands with real pleasure. He had laughed then, too. And so had Sarah. They had both laughed; they were too old. But then the greatest memory of all flooded the old man's head. It had happened! They *did* have a child—a son all right—and the whole camp had hooted for joy. Sarah and Abraham had led the laughter, their prune faces wrinkled into crackling smiles. They all had laughed so hard that when it came time to name the child, there was only one name by which to call him. He was Isaac, the child of laughter, the child of old age, the child of the promise of God!

Finally, we reach our text! It has been important to set the context for the test. If the stories are not known prior to the test, it will lose its unique surprise, shock, and mystery. Note that I have tried to give the birth of Isaac a sense of joy, fun, and finality so that the test will be felt by the hearers in all its power. All seems ready for a happy ending, but the text of the day first must lead its hearers in other directions. The sense of ease in the story is about to be shattered.

Abraham got up to look once again at the child Isaac. Then a familiar voice split the night. "Abraham! Abraham!" "Here I am," the old man replied. He knew it was God. "Take your son," God said. "Which one?" the old man thought. God answered, "Your only son." "But both are only sons—one of Sarah, one of Hagar," he thought. "Isaac whom you love," God said. Ah, Isaac, the child of laughter, the child of my old age. "Go to the land of seeing, and offer *him* there as a burnt offering on one of the mountains," God instructed. The silence returned, and the old man remembered God's word of long ago: "Go to a land. Leave what you love." Without a word the old man went to his tent and fell into a deep sleep.

In this brief section I try to highlight the multiple surprises of the text. God's awesome request comes without overt explanation, but it does come with clear memory—a memory I emphasized earlier in the sermon. Abraham has heard this voice and a similar request before. Before he has gone without a word. Since that time, he has done many things to make us wonder what he will do this time. I try to make his reaction to God's call as simple as possible to heighten the surprise of it. Now the text can practically tell itself.

Abraham rose at first light, saddled his donkey, and called for his two servants to hurry. He took Isaac, too. Abraham then cut the wood needed for the sacrifice and left for the "place of seeing" that God had told him about. Three days passed. Then Abraham raised his eyes and saw the place of seeing in the distance. He said to his servants, "You two stay here with the donkey. I and the boy will go up there, and we will worship; then we will return to you." And with no further word, Abraham took the wood of the sacrifice and laid it on Isaac, his son. He took in his own hand the flint to start the fire and his old knife. They went together.

Isaac was the first to break the silence. "My father," he cried. "Here I am, my son," Abraham answered. "I see fire and wood,

A PURE NARRATIVE SERMON: THE BEST LAUGH OF ALL

but where is the lamb for a burnt offering?" Isaac asked. Isaac said nothing about the knife. Abraham said, "God will see to a lamb for a burnt offering, my son." They went together.

The text itself reveals how right the words are—how balanced and powerful their expression is. It seems best in this case, then, to preserve nearly verbatim that expression. Note, however, certain additions to improve understanding. I read Moriah as "seeing" to take advantage of the theme of seeing that is so prominent in the story. I also add some lines about silence and the breaking of silence to emphasize the heaviness of the dialogue. I remind the hearer of the knife by pointing out that Isaac said nothing about it in his catalogue of the items for the sacrifice. When Abraham's response to Isaac is spoken, I suggest a slight pause between "offering" and "my son" to provide the hearer the chance to hear the terrible ambiguity of the expression. Note, too, that I have highlighted Isaac in the midst of the activity of Abraham in the same way that Genesis 22:6 does.

They came to the place. Abraham built the altar and laid the wood in order. He tied Isaac, his son, and laid him on the altar. He took his old knife to kill his son. But again the silence was broken—this time by a heavenly voice. "Abraham! Abraham!" The old man answered as he had twice before, "Here I am." "Don't do anything at all to the boy, because now I know that you truly worship God. After all, you have not withheld your son, your only son, from me." Abraham looked behind him and saw a ram trapped in the bushes. He offered the ram as a sacrifice instead of his son. The angel spoke again, "This great deed shows that God was right about you all along. And so God will make your descendants like sand, like the stars, which are beyond number."

So Abraham called the place "God sees." Some people call it "A place where God is seen." But Abraham knew that both names are correct. He knew that God was seen on that mountain, but he also knew that God had seen him and seen to the promise—a promise that nothing can defer, deflect, or destroy.

Abraham left the place of seeing, and news came to him that his closest relatives were having children so fast that they could hardly be named or counted. The old man merely smiled; it was God seeing to it. It was God fulfilling the promise. And as he thought back to the lying, the disbelief, and the weak human efforts to help God along, the old man's face cracked a wider smile, which grew into a chuckle, which emerged as a guffaw, which turned into a great belly laugh—a laugh that split the silence. Perhaps you can hear it even now. It is a laugh of obedience—obedience out of a conviction of things not seen. And that is the best laugh of all.

As the most dramatic part of the story approaches—the attempted sacrifice—I suggest that the pace of the delivery be increased to hurl the hearer toward the fact that Abraham is willing and ready to do it. He will sacrifice his son in obedience to God. When the angel intrudes into the scene, the preacher should muster all of the drama at his or her command. After the angel's announcement, I use the narrative's own movement—the second call of the angel and the numerous birth stories of Abraham's relatives—to suggest that the obedience of the old man has gained the favor of God and has brought about the promised results: astonishingly numerous progeny. I close with a return to the motif of laughter. Earlier in the story laughter was a sign of disobedience; now it is an emblem of joyful obedience—an emblem that I highlight with a reference to the familiar definition of faith, based on obedience, found in Hebrews 11:1. That obedience provides the best laugh of all.

◆ ◆ ◆

The content and the form of this pure narrative sermon are mirrored in the biblical story. I tried to allow a narrative reading of the story to inform the way I proceeded at every step. First, the basic concern that I found in my reading—the obedience of Abraham—informed my sermon from beginning to end; I attempted to make all parts of the narrative serve that end, from descriptions to dialogues. Second, the movement of the biblical narrative, its subtle details and its more obvious shape, found their way into my telling. Of course, I could not include everything unearthed in a literary analysis. To do so would tax the ears of even the most engaged listener! But my reading directly generated my preaching, and that is the goal of narrative preaching. In that sense, this kind of preaching is potentially the most thoroughly biblical kind. Third, I used my imagination to enliven the telling at certain

84

points, both for clarity and for interest. The motif of laughter became central as a memorable way to characterize Abraham and Sarah and to indicate how the changing meaning of that laughter mirrors the change in Abraham from obedience to disobedience to obedience. His final great laugh in the sermon is an attempt to leave the listener with that picture of the joy of radical obedience as seen in a chortling old man.

SOME NARRATIVE NOTES TO THE SERMON

Plot

My narrative sermon "The Best Laugh of All" makes several assumptions about plot. First, I consider Genesis 22 to be the climax of the story of Abraham that began at the end of Genesis 11. More specifically, the grammatical and thematic structure of Genesis 12:1 and Genesis 22:2 are identical. The construction *lek l'kah,* "you take," occurs only at these two places in the Hebrew Bible. Thus, the reader is drawn into a comparison of the two stories. In chapter 12 Abraham is asked to leave everything he knows to go to a place that he has never seen. So it is in chapter 22. Here Abraham is asked to leave not only a physical location but also to leave his certainty in the promise of God—a certainty that is wrapped up in the child, Isaac, for whom he and Sarah have waited so long. The apparent climax of the story—the birth of Isaac in chapter 21—is, in fact, no climax at all. The concern of the story is not with Isaac but with Abraham. The plot tells me that I must focus on him in my narration.

My second assumption is that there really *is* a plot in this story of Abraham. It is commonplace in the study of these chapters to demonstrate the multiple origins of the chapters that make up the narrative of Genesis 12–22. It is generally agreed that three of the so-called documentary sources of the Pentateuch may be found here: J, E, and P. This is a likely assumption. Still, there is a plot, a dynamic sequence of action, created out of these disparate sources, beginning with Abraham's marriage to a barren woman (Gen. 11:30) and their subsequent call from God to be a "great nation." Thus, the tension of the plot is established: how are Abraham and Sarah to become a great nation when they are incapable of producing even a single heir? Their attempts to do so on their own lead to domestic disaster (Gen. 16:1-14 and Gen. 21:8-21) and to political divisions fraught with danger (Gen. 16:12).

As the main lines of the plot are interwoven around the issue of the lack of an heir, the theme of an increasing incredulity on the part of both Abraham and Sarah is introduced. Abraham goes readily in response to God's first command (Gen. 12:1-3), and is said to "believe Yahweh" (Gen. 15:6). But as the time without an heir grows ever longer, Abraham laughs loudly at God's reiteration of the promised son (Gen. 17:17), and Sarah adds her own unbelieving laughter, although it is a laugh she intended only for herself. God, however, hears her laugh as clearly as Abraham's raucous chortle.

The response of God to all of this laughter is to give a son to the aged couple, whose unbelieving laughter now becomes the joyous laughter of children (Gen. 21:6). The child is named Isaac, which is Hebrew for "laughter." What else would one call a child birthed by a ninety-year-old woman? But the laughter soon stops as the surprising God speaks once again at the beginning of chapter 22. The narrator says, "after these things" (Gen. 22:1), and the reader is thus urged to recall the plot that has preceded the coming announcement.

My third assumption about the plot is focused more narrowly on chapter 22. This story is about *Abraham*, not Isaac, or even God. The plot makes this fact clear. It is Abraham to whom God and the angel speak. It is Abraham who acts in the story; all other characters are acted upon. It is Abraham who closes the story, who leaves the mountain of the sacrifice alone. Isaac completely disappears from the plot. Thus, plot tells me that the narration *must* be focused on Abraham, if I am to be true to the Bible's own narration.

Whenever reading the narratives of the Hebrew Bible, we must take careful account of the plot before doing any detailed work on those narratives. One practical way to determine whether or not you understand the plot is to tell the story in your own words to someone who is willing to listen. If no one is available, tell your story into a tape recorder. Listen carefully to determine whether the plot is clear and forceful. Your telling will be clear enough when it is understandable to a child, at least in its broad outlines.

Character and Characterization

As was noted in chapter 2, biblical narrators characterize the persons in their stories in two primary ways: what the characters *do* and what the characters *say*. The portrayal of Abraham illustrates these ways.

The Actions of Abraham

Abraham listens attentively as God demands that he offer his son Isaac as a burnt offering on a mysterious mountain that Abraham has never seen. He reacts to God's call by going, without comment. The verb used at the beginning of verse 3 of chapter 22 indicates eagerness and haste (see, for example, Judg. 19:5,8; I Sam. 15:12,29). When addressing Abraham's response to this amazing request, many commentators have provided various psychological explanations for his behavior. In a much-quoted article about this scene, Erich Auerbach says, "Bitter to him is the early morning in which he saddles his ass." He later comments, "his soul is torn between desperate rebellion and hopeful expectation."[1] Likewise John Skinner speaks of his "desperation" and "conflict."[2] Even Kenneth R. R. Gros Louis, who rejects Auerbach's psychologizing as "solely a twentieth-century interpretation," finds Abraham "tense and anxious" because he is about to discover once and for all whether or not "the Lord's covenant with him concerning Isaac's descendants is true or not."[3]

Such motivations, however, seem unlikely to be behind Abraham's silent obedience to the command of his God. Abraham's silence is perhaps more significant and truer to the content of the narration.[4] The reader does not expect Abraham to be silent at this point in the story. Abraham's key attribute before this climactic scene is his loquaciousness. In chapter 12, for example, it is the talkative Abraham who schemes with a completely silent Sarai to attempt to bamboozle the pharaoh. Likewise, in chapter 18 (and later in chapter 23), Abraham loves a good bargain—even when God is the bargaining partner. So why is Abraham silent now? We cannot answer this question by asking ourselves what we would think or feel if God were to ask such a thing of us. That would run the risk of missing the actual fact of the narration. What we can say is that Abraham's silence is quite deafening, and it is not surprising

87

that so many have rushed into that silence with explanations. Although we simply do not know why Abraham has nothing to say at this point in the story, we can learn from his silence. One thing we learn from his silence as it is contrasted to his loquaciousness—as I have done in my sermon "The Best Laugh of All"—is that the story has a quality of unexpectedness.

Although Abraham's willingness to sacrifice his son may be unexpected behavior, Abraham's silence and purposeful actions clearly indicate that he is determined to be obedient to his God. As the rather perfunctory verse 4 of chapter 22 illustrates—with its silent and rapid progress to the mysterious mountain—Abraham *is* going to perform the deed asked of him. Abraham's silence and direct movement toward the spot create the picture of a man on a mission. Once Abraham has prepared the altar, he silently lays the child on the altar, takes his knife, and prepares to carry out the sacrifice. Indeed, *all* of his actions and *all* of his silences portray an Abraham ready to follow the will of God. With a judicious and sparing use of scenic description, the narrator has offered the reader a picture of a man of perfect obedience.

This portrayal requires that we must be convinced that Abraham is willing and ready to do the deed. He is not dissembling. He is not expecting to be released from the task. The miraculous appearance of the angel and the ram in the bush are as much a surprise for Abraham as they are for us. We can be sure of this because of the import of the word *test* found in verse 1. This word is used in significant places in the Hebrew Bible to indicate to the one setting the test—usually God—whether or not those being tested are faithful. Because one may be faithful to the test or fail the test, we can be sure that the test is real.[5] Abraham certainly is faithful to the test.

Because Abraham's test is real, the narrator rivets our attention on Abraham, the object of the test. Will he pass? What will happen if he fails? How does this test relate to the promise of God, a promise made concrete in the life of Isaac? All of these scenic characterizations make it clear that my pure narrative sermon must have Abraham as the chief actor, and that my portrayal of him must focus on the question of obedience. What Abraham says reinforces these conclusions.

A PURE NARRATIVE SERMON: THE BEST LAUGH OF ALL

Abraham's Speeches

The speeches of Abraham in chapter 22 are brief but very important for his characterization. His first words are the same as his last. In response to God's initial call he says, "Here I am," and when stopped by the voice of God's angel, he says again, "Here I am." The Hebrew could also be read, "Behold me" or "Look at me." Abraham presents himself as one ready to hear and obey.

When Abraham, his son, and the servants arrive at the mountain, he says to them, "You both stay here with the ass, while I and the boy go up there. We will worship, then we will return to you." This speech of Abraham is quite vague and thus misleading. He tells them that he and "the boy" (the same word used to describe the servants) are going "up there" (the RSV translates this "yonder"). Abraham objectifies his son, refusing to call him by his name. "We will worship," he continues evasively, "and we will return to you." Not only is Isaac not named, but the kind of worship anticipated is also hidden. The promise is that both will return in due course. The servants may be duped, but we the readers cannot be, because we know Abraham's purpose.

This is a classic illustration of dramatic irony. The reader knows more than certain characters in the story know, and so the narrator affords us both the pleasures and pains of our superior knowledge. One is reminded here of Oedipus. The oracle warns Oedipus that he will murder his father and marry his mother. To Oedipus, the possibility of such events seems ludicrous, but we watch in rising horror as the oracle's words astonishingly come true. Aristotle, in his insightful commentary on the play, suggested that Sophocles thus heightened our pity for the hero by letting us in on his fate. The difference between Oedipus and Abraham, of course, is that Oedipus stumbles blindly, caught in the inexorable web of the gods, while Abraham moves purposefully to perform the command of his God. Yet our identity with Abraham remains strong, due to the device of dramatic irony.

Abraham's next speech is uttered in response to his son. He says to Isaac what he has said to God in verse 2 and what he will say to the angel of God in verse 11: "Here I am." Abraham will do what God asks, but because God's request is primary for him, he cannot do precisely what Isaac asks. Thus, when Isaac wants to know, "where is the lamb for the burnt offering," Abraham's reply is less than forthcoming. "God will see to it, a sheep for the whole burnt offering, my son." Everett Fox suggests that we might replace the comma after the word "offering" with a dash to capture the irony of the phrase.[6] When the son himself *is* the sacrifice, the irony cuts deeply, and we, with our special knowledge of the scene, are cut deeply as well.

Abraham's two less-than-truthful speeches are framed by his absolute stance of obedience before God and God's messenger. Thus, Abraham's dissembling to the servants and to his son is done so that he may be obedient to the call of God. Compare these "white lies" to the sniveling untruths of chapters 12 and 20. In the former, Abraham lies plainly to save his own life at the expense of Sarai and of the promise of God: "Say that you are my sister, so that it may go well with me because of you, and that my life may be spared on your account" (Gen. 12:13). When he is caught in the lie by pharaoh, he falls silent. In the latter, Abraham has much to say in his own defense, when Abimelech discovers that Sarah is Abraham's wife, but that defense rings hollow. He first claims he lied because he thought that "there was no fear of God in this place." Such a response has a religious "sound" to it, but the reason for the lie remains the same: Abraham was trying to save his own skin at the expense of his wife (Gen. 20:11). He then adds that Sarah really *is* his sister—his half-sister, that is. This news is designed to make everything all right, but it must seem late in the game to Abimelech for Abraham to reveal the relationship. After all, Abimelech's very life is under threat because of Abraham's lie about Sarah. Whereas Abraham's lies in chapters 12 and 20 are clearly self-serving and hence disobedient, his partial untruths in chapter 22 *add* to the portrait of a fully obedient Abraham—a man whose one goal is now to follow his God in all things, even when that God seems to ask what is patently absurd.

In both speech and scene, in both silence and action, the narrator portrays, in Abraham, a man of obedience. My narrative sermon "The Best Laugh of All" emphasizes this obvious fact of the narration, as I have read it. Because the narrator's means of characterization are so sure, so persuasive, I often merely borrowed what has been done in order to make my own portrayal of Abraham.

Point of View

The use of point of view in the narrative is designed to emphasize the goals of the narration uncovered in the analysis of plot and characterization. Accordingly, the author fixes our attention on Abraham from the beginning. He is at the center of all action and all speech. Indeed, every speech is either directed to Abraham or spoken by him. Even at the end of chapter 22, when the promise of God for numerous progeny is being fulfilled in Abraham's relatives, it is Abraham himself who is told about the wonderful births (Gen. 22:20-24). The only time that Abraham is not the sole focus of action or speech is in the small phrase found at the end of verse 6. After he tells his half-truth to the servants, the narrator allows the reader to assume the point of view of the servants as they watch Abraham and his son ascend the mountain: "So they went both of them together." It is a brief respite, however, because we soon catch up with father and son and overhear the dialogue between them about God's provision for the proper sacrifice. When the author repeats the phrase "so they went both of them together" after the dialogue, there is an added poignancy. As far as we and Abraham know, this togetherness soon will be sundered by the stroke of Abraham's knife.

Where does the reader stand in relationship to the story? Because it is a narration in the third person—that is, we are told this story by a narrator—we stand outside and watch the unfolding of the action. However, we cannot remain fully objective because the narrator has allowed us, at least part of the way, into the house of narration. We know—as Abraham, the servants, and Isaac do not—that this is a test of God. Furthermore, we know—as the servants and Isaac do not, but as Abraham does—that Abraham is ready to sacrifice his son to fulfill the command of God. Thus, the author manipulates our relationship to the account by letting us inside while at the same time rendering us powerless to alter the course of the events unfolding inexorably before our eyes. In these ways, our emotions are engaged perhaps more than our intellects. Such is the power of point of view in narration.

Clues Toward the Narrative Sermon

My reading of the narrative led to the conclusion that the main actor of this drama is Abraham and that the chief interest of the narrator in telling this story is obedience to the promise of God. The story is about the quality of Abraham's faith. When I determined this emphasis, I thought immediately of the memorable definition of faith found in the letter to the Hebrews (11:1), which would make a fitting conclusion to the story. Often I compose my narrative sermons backwards, beginning with the conclusion to provide myself with a certain goal and direction for my telling.

After determining the emphasis and conclusion, I then settled on the controlling metaphor for the sermon: laughter. Within the longer story of Abraham, laughter moved from a sign of disobedience to a sign of the presence of the promise of God in the person of the child of laughter, Isaac. Therefore I used laughter to tie the story together.

Because the text was Genesis 22, the last chapter of a longer story, I decided to tell the context of the main plot as the flashback of an old man sitting by a campfire. The phrase, "after these things," gave me the clue for this move.

Once these things were determined, I had direction, goal, and some basic sense of the means to achieve the goal. Then, I was ready to employ some of the discoveries I had made in my analysis of plot, character, and point of view. I could not use them all; too much detail could submerge the word. Yet the wonderful details of the narration are what bring the story to fuller life.

A FRAME NARRATIVE SERMON:
GOD, THE MOABITE WIDOW

Their arms and hands formed beautiful shapes in the air. They were about fifteen in number—black and white, young and old, male and female. Like most church choirs, their faces were alight with the joy of music. But they were not like most church choirs; all fifteen were deaf. For the first time in my life, I was *watching* a choir perform rather than listening to one. It was a beautiful experience, but a disconcerting one.

After the performance the director, a young hearing woman, told a story about one of the choir's members. Several years before, a young man had rushed into the director's office, greatly agitated and crying. The boy had only recently been adopted by hearing parents. His new parents were making loving attempts to enter the silent world of their new son. But on this particular day, things obviously were not going well. He signed hurriedly, "I can't go home any more! My parents know I am deaf, and they know the signs pretty well, but they look at me as if I were some kind of freak or something. But I am still me; I just can't hear!" After the boy and the director had communicated some more, the boy calmed down. The conversation turned to theological matters. The boy signed, "Does God know the signs?" The director signed in response. "Oh, of course. Didn't you know? God is deaf."

God is deaf? Could it be? Why, how would God hear my prayers, how would God be "enthroned on the praises" of the people if the Divine One could not even hear those praises? It was an outrageous notion! But immediately I thought of another story which helped me to see things anew.

In this frame narrative I use the opening story of the deaf choir to intro-duce the idea of unexpected perception, an important idea that I uncov-ered in my reading of Ruth. In my telling of the Ruth story, I propose to emphasize Ruth, the amazingly devoted one, who through her devotion brought about the wholeness of her adopted community. However, the fact that it is Ruth—the Moabite widow attempting to live in a thor-oughly patriarchal culture—who offers this kind of devotion gives the story its own sharp angle of vision that focuses our attention on the unexpected one.

The opening story also alerts the hearer that Ruth is somehow going to provide an image of God that will offer the surprise of the new and the fresh and may provide the hearer with fresh resources for thinking about God. God, in addition to being deaf for the young choir boy, will be a Moabite widow in this telling of Ruth.

It is the time when the judges are judging. A man who lived in Bethlehem—Elimelech by name—leaves home with his wife, Naomi, and their two sons because of a terrible famine in the land of Judah. Now this is not an easy time to go traveling. With tricky murderers like Ehud; crazy would-be kings like Abimelech; wild, over-sexed brutes like Samson; and rash child-killers like Jephthah populating the land, it is no wonder that the book about their exploits summa-rizes the times with this phrase: "Everyone did what was right in their own eyes." Nevertheless, Elimelech and his family travel to the land of Moab. Moab may not be the best place to go; after all, the Israelites remember that the Moabites exist only because of the inces-tuous relationship between Lot and one of his lusty daughters. Still, David sent his parents to live in Moab for a time while he and Saul fought it out, so maybe the place is not all bad.

But it does not take very long for things to go bad. First, Elim-elech dies and leaves Naomi a widow. A widow in the ancient world is no easy position. Without a husband, a woman is cut off from the culture's spoken and unspoken concern; her religious, social, and economic rights are seriously impaired. She falls rapidly to the bottom of the social ladder, being classed with orphans, strangers, and foreigners. But, at least Naomi still has her strapping Israelite sons; they provide a male link to the culture. After some years, however, the sons marry Moabite women, one named Orpah and the other named Ruth. Well, one could hardly blame them; they are young and eligible and living in Moab. Naomi does not seem to mind their marriages, and they all continue to live in the foreign land.

Then tragedy strikes again. Both of the lads die, and the Moabite scene becomes a very different one—a far emptier one. Now there are *three* widows, two of whom are Moabite. Talk about a famine! A lack of food in the physical realm is matched by a lack of prospects in the domestic realm. Word finally reaches Naomi that the famine in Israel is easing, and she determines to head home. She moves slowly and painfully, her slumped shoulders draped with the sorrow of three male deaths. Behind her, at a respectful distance, follow Orpah and Ruth.

> *In this first scene I do two things. First, I provide the hearer with the necessary names and information so that the story can begin. Second, and most importantly, I provide background to the information, background that original hearers would have known and that could have been assumed by the narrator. My modern hearers must be told about the conditions for widows in the ancient world, must be reminded of the nature of the time of the Judges, and must be informed of the place called Moab. All of this information gives the proper tone to the story. However, all of this information must be offered unobtrusively and lightly, so as not to disturb the narrative.*
>
> *Another thing I try to do as I begin is to introduce some of the themes that will recur as the sermon progresses. I emphasize the theme of famine and emptiness that is central to the story. Also, I begin my portrayal of Naomi as a woman so overwhelmed by personal disaster that she will miss completely the great gift that Ruth will offer of herself. Hence, I show Naomi's slow movement back to Judah.*
>
> *I also take every opportunity to employ details in the sermon that can be unearthed in a narrative reading. For example, I use the word* lad *to describe Naomi's dead sons, because this word was used in the text and will recur at the end of the story when the "lad" is born to Ruth. The integrity of the story is thus further enhanced and shared with the hearers.*

Naomi comes out of her sad reverie long enough to see the two Moabites following her, and she swiftly urges them to return to their mothers' homes. She thanks them for their kindness to her and to her dead sons and expresses her hopes that God will help them to find new homes in the houses of their second husbands. In short, Naomi paints for the two women a bright picture of the possibilities of life for them in Moab. The implication is that life in Israel with Naomi holds no such promise.

But the two women refuse to return, and through their tears they insist on returning with Naomi to her people. Naomi shares the impossibilities of life for them in Israel. "There are laws and customs in my country," she says, "that insist that a widow is to marry her dead husband's closest relative in order to keep the male line alive in the land." Naomi then offers an absurd scenario designed to indicate that their fulfillment of these laws and customs is out of the question. "I am too old to have another husband," she says. "Even if I had one on this very night [ridiculous!], and somehow became pregnant by him [impossible!], would you wait for the little boy [assuming it was a boy!] to grow up and marry him? Would you not marry someone else before you got too old yourselves? No, my daughters, it is all too absurd. It is far more bitter for me than for you that the hand of God has gone forth against me."

Well, that is enough for Orpah. She takes the sensible road back to the place of possibility for her—Moab. "But Ruth clung to her." The verb *clung* is a very strong and intimate one. We read it in Genesis: "That is why a man leaves his father and mother and *clings* to his woman and they become one flesh." Ruth now clings to Naomi, and Naomi is very surprised—as we are—and perhaps even a bit disgusted. "Look, your sister has gone back to her people and her gods; go join her!" What she means is, "You are showing poor decision-making skills, woman; use your head!" It is quite clear that Naomi wants nothing whatsoever to do with Ruth. And that makes Ruth's next speech all the more astonishing.

"Do not force me to abandon you or to return from following you. I will go with you, lodge with you; your people and your God will be mine. I will even share your grave. Why, may the Lord do something awful to me if even death separates me from you." There is nothing sensible about this speech. There is no place in Israel for Ruth. She is a woman—strike one. She is a widow— strike two. She is a foreigner—strike three. Besides, Naomi has no interest in Ruth no matter how kind and devoted she may be. Ruth, in effect, has thrown her life away for her mother-in-law in her memorable address. It is no wonder that this speech has lived in the memories of so many readers for so many centuries. It is an unequalled example of devotion with no expectation of any sort of return. Earlier Naomi urged God to deal with Ruth as Ruth had dealt with Naomi and her dead husband. In other words, Naomi hoped that God would act like Ruth. She said more than she knew when she said that.

In the face of this speech, Naomi is shocked into silence. Ruth is not to be dissuaded. So both continue the journey to Bethlehem. Upon their arrival, the entire community is excited and thrilled to see them, especially to see their old friend, Naomi, whom they have not seen for so many years. "Is it really Naomi, the pleasant one?" they shout with enthusiasm. "No!" says the bitter old woman. "Don't call me 'pleasant.' Call me rather 'Mara,' the bitter one. God has made me very bitter. I went away full, but the Lord has brought me back empty!" What must the now-silent Ruth think of that? She just gave her life for this woman; now the woman has announced to everyone that her life is completely empty. Ruth is herself abandoned, alone, in a foreign land. Perhaps now she will at last take the sensible course and return to Moab. But if we believe that, we have not listened to Ruth nor have we believed her when she spoke to Naomi on the Bethlehem road. This woman will *never* abandon Naomi. Thus ends act one of the drama.

Having laid the groundwork in the opening section, I now can practically allow the story to tell itself. I need only follow where the text leads, allowing the details discovered to sound their distinctive notes. Because that text urges us to keep our attention on the selfless devotion of Ruth, I, as sermon narrator, try to keep that thrust of the narrative uppermost in the hearer's mind. To do that, I must break into the story as narrator and emphasize my special concern so that it does not get lost under the telling of the story itself. I try to equate the actions of Ruth with the actions of God and to highlight the truly astonishing behavior of Ruth in every way that I can.

As you will note, I paraphrase Ruth's famous speech. I do this because I do not want the very familiar words to be lost in their familiarity. However, I believe that the familiar words themselves can take on added power if they are placed in their proper context in the story. You must decide which will work better for you.

As the curtain rises on act two, a new character is introduced. The first thing we learn about him is that he is one of Naomi's closest relatives by marriage—a potential marriage partner for Ruth! Not only is he properly related to fulfill the laws and customs of the land, but he also is a man of substance—a man of value, virtue, and property. His name is Boaz. But Ruth knows nothing of his existence, and Naomi apparently has forgotten about him in her despair.

Ruth turns to her sullen mother-in-law and announces that she will go out to glean in the field of an Israelite from whom she hopes to find favor. For the second time, Ruth is risking her life for her mother-in-law. To glean in ancient Israel is to participate in the welfare system. The law states that as the fields are harvested, the harvesters are not to cut the grain right to the edges of the field but are to leave the grain at the edges for the poor, the stranger, the orphan, and the widow. Furthermore, when grain falls out of the bundles as they are being bound up, the harvesters are to leave the fallen grain for the same outcasts. Gleaning is a difficult and demeaning way to stay alive, and it is often dangerous, especially for a young and unknown foreign widow. Ruth could be at the mercy of lusty field hands or hard-bitten field-owners. Nonetheless, she goes to glean, because Naomi must be cared for. And as chance would have it, she goes right to the part of the field that belongs to Boaz.

Just at that moment Boaz returns from Bethlehem and greets his workers with a hearty, "The Lord be with you!" They all respond, "The Lord bless you!" Everybody likes Boaz! But he has something else on his mind. Looking at Ruth he says, "To whom does this woman belong?" The worker who is questioned tells Boaz that she is the same Moabite who returned with Naomi from Moab and that she has asked to glean in his fields. Ruth, in effect, belongs to no one. Boaz takes special interest in her, warning her to stay close to his working women and to drink some water from that drawn by his working men. He has carefully warned his men to leave her alone. Ruth is surprised by his interest. All she wanted was a day of rough gleaning, but she has stumbled into a field where the owner speaks of her staying only there and offers her the privilege of drinking with the paid Israelite workers. It is a bit much!

But Boaz knows more about Ruth than he first revealed. He says to Ruth, "All that you have done for your mother-in-law since the death of your husband has been told me, and how you abandoned father and mother and native land to come to a people that you did not know before." Boaz is the first person to know what we know of Ruth. She is a powerhouse of true devotion, and Boaz is fully in awe of her. He calls for God to grant her a "full reward" for this great act of devotion. Ruth is comforted and showered with kindness by his words, but she still remains at a loss to explain his amazing interest in her.

But Boaz goes even further. At lunch, he invites her to eat with him, and he passes extra portions of food to her. After she returns to work, he tells his workers to allow her to glean even among the already bound-up bundles, which are strictly off-limits to gleaners. Even more boldly, he demands that his workers pull some grain out of some of the bundles and leave it within her easy reach. He definitely wants to make Ruth's workday as easy and profitable as possible.

I trust that you can see what Boaz is doing. If you cannot, you need to have your heart checked—and I do not mean with an EKG machine! The old boy is falling in love! But he is reticent—unwilling to declare his intentions openly to the woman who has awed him so. But he will use all of the tricks he can to bind her to him.

The tricks work. She finishes a day of gleaning with a huge amount of barley, perhaps as much as forty-five pounds. With this great cache of grain, Ruth returns to Naomi, first offering to her the remains of the generous lunch she had with Boaz. Naomi catches sight of the pile of grain and shouts, "Where did you glean today? Where did you work? Blessed be the man who noticed you! I never saw a glean like that!" Ruth answers Naomi by saying, "The man with whom I worked today is named Boaz. May he be blessed by the Lord, who has not abandoned the living or the dead." Naomi cries, "The man is a relative of ours, one of our possible redeemers." We can hear in Naomi's excitement the beginning of a plan to get Ruth and Boaz together. But if she expects the reticent Boaz to act, she is mistaken. Each day Ruth gets up to glean until the end of both the barley and wheat harvests, which is at least seven long weeks. Boaz' initial interest in Ruth apparently is not sustained. Act two ends in disappointment.

Act two is so well written that little intrusion is necessary to sustain my reading of the story. I feel it important to note only Naomi's unconscious tying together of Ruth and God (Ruth 2:20), because that is one of the important themes of this reading. I add a bit of humor as I emphasize Naomi's great excitement over the truly stupendous size of Ruth's one-day glean. I do think this surprise is implied by the text. Also, Boaz' growing love for Ruth and his backhanded way of expressing it allow room for some comedy as he brings his workers in on his less-than-subtle attempts to keep Ruth in his field. As I note, his subterfuge also denotes an extreme reticence—whether out of shyness or fear or excessive propriety we cannot know, which makes necessary the outlandish plot of act three. Thus, a clear telling of act two is very important to the shape of the whole story.

Naomi has waited long enough. So, as act three begins, she announces her plan. As we probably can guess, the plan will include Ruth, but not even Ruth can imagine what Naomi is about to ask her to do. "My daughter, I must seek a home for you, so that all may be well with you. Boaz is our near relative. He is this very night winnowing barley at the threshing floor near the gate of the city. He is a good man, but not too forthcoming. Therefore, take a long bath, using my best perfumes. Put on your finest dress—you know the one—and go down to the threshing floor. Don't reveal yourself to the man, but watch where he lies down to go to sleep. After you are certain that he is asleep, walk quietly over to him, uncover his legs, and lie down next to him. He will tell you what to do." Use fine perfumes, put on your finest dress, uncover him, lie down beside him. Naomi clearly has sexual entrapment in mind! In other words, if Boaz won't come to you, then you must go to him. And if you throw yourself at him, he will be forced to "tell you what to do." Without a single comment, Ruth agrees to this astonishing scheme: "All that you say I will do." But she doesn't, as we shall see.

Oh, Ruth bathes, anoints, and dresses all right. She goes secretly to the threshing floor all right. She sneaks over to the sleeping Boaz, uncovers his legs, and lies down all right. And when he stirs in his sleep and awakens to find a woman in his bed, he shouts in alarm, "Who are you?" Ruth coolly replies, "I am Ruth, your handmaid." Now, if Ruth had stopped there and waited for Boaz to tell her what to do, she would have done just what her mother-in-law told her. But we ought to know by now that this woman is not likely to wait to be told what to do by anyone. So, she presses right on in great boldness. "Spread your wing over your handmaid, for you are a redeemer," she says. Now if that is not a wedding invitation, I do not know what it is!

Boaz recognizes immediately what Ruth is asking, and he blesses her for choosing him over younger men, whether poor or rich. He then says what we already know—that Ruth is running the show. "I will do for you all that you ask," he says. Ruth's bold risk and devotion apparently have paid off at last. We witness a romantic tryst on the threshing floor at midnight. What possibly could spoil the imminent marriage between Ruth and Boaz? Only one thing. . . .

"It is true," says Boaz, "that I am a close relative and can play the role of redeemer for you; however, there is a relative who is a closer relation than I." Like a thunderclap Boaz drops the news that there is an unnamed man who has prior rights to the property of Naomi's dead husband—property that includes Ruth. Now the romantic scene is overshadowed by the specter of this new redeemer. Midnight on the threshing floor is now fraught with danger, for the relationship between Boaz and Ruth possibly is illegal and certainly is against the customs and mores of the community.

In fearful whispers, Boaz vows to play the role of redeemer as long as the nearer redeemer agrees not to do so. He urges Ruth, nonetheless, to lie down until the morning. She does so, but she awakens to go before any light edges the sky. Before she goes, Boaz fills her apron with grain as a token of his love and commitment. As Ruth walks back into the city, holding the two corners of her apron bursting with grain, she looks as if she were pregnant with Boaz' child—a lovely presage for things to come. Boaz, meanwhile, rushes to the gate of the city to settle the legal tangle before anyone can find out about the night on the threshing floor.

As Ruth approaches Naomi, the old woman anxiously asks about events on the threshing floor. Ruth tells her all the man did for her and claims that Boaz gave her the load of grain so that she did not have to go back empty-handed to her mother-in-law. Boaz, of course, said nothing of the kind, but in *all* things the devoted Ruth has Naomi uppermost in her mind. Naomi assures Ruth that

Boaz will not wait a moment but will get everything arranged this very day. So Act III ends in tension and hope.

> *Act three needs even less intrusion than act two. Again the story is so well written that it carries its own weight. I will offer a word of advice about the way in which sexual talk and action should be handled in a narrative sermon. As always, use the biblical storyteller as your guide. Never make explicit what is offered only implicitly. The threshing floor scene is veiled in ambiguity. The narrator neither says nor denies that sexual activity is part of the scene. Likewise, the preacher should only suggest, allowing the hearers to conclude for themselves what they think is going on. In that way, the hearers have the pleasure of active involvement in the story and the preacher cannot be accused of being sexually explicit in the pulpit. Your goal is to activate their imaginations so that they can fill out the scene in whatever ways their imaginations lead them.*

Naomi is right. Even as she speaks to Ruth, Boaz is standing in the gate of the city. As the sun peeks over the horizon, he catches sight of the unnamed "nearer redeemer" and calls out to him, "Turn aside, you so-and-so, and sit down." The man does so. Boaz then calls together ten male elders to judge the case. Boaz offers Mr. So-and-so the right to purchase some property. He says: "Naomi, just returned from Moab, is selling a piece of land which belonged to our mutual kinsman, Elimelech. I thought I would tell you of it and offer you the chance to buy it in the presence of those assembled. If you will redeem it, then redeem it. But if not, tell me so that I can redeem it, because I come after you."

Do you notice something missing from this speech? That's right, there is no mention of Ruth! In fact, it is the first time that any piece of property is brought into consideration at all. But Mr. So-and-so is intrigued and pleased by the prospect of more property; he readily agrees to play the role of redeemer. "Oh, by the way," continues Boaz; "the day you buy the property, you are buying Ruth, the Moabite woman, in order to restore the name of her dead husband upon his inheritance." Well, that is another kettle of fish entirely to Mr. So-and-so. It is one thing to inherit the care and upkeep of one old widow, who can't live forever. Surely her property would more than compensate for any needs she might have. But a *young* widow, whose first child would inherit

102

the property and whose possible other children could bankrupt a man by their incessant demands—no, it was more than a sensible, fiscally responsible man should take on. Mr. So-and-so rejects his right of redemption and goes home, mumbling something about debits and credits all the way. Like Orpah in act one, Mr. So-and-so chooses the expected, the easy, and the sensible.

Boaz is at last free to announce his intention to buy the property of Elimelech, property in which he has not the slightest interest. He, of course, wants only the incredible Ruth to be his wife. In ringing patriarchal tones, he says that he has *bought* property and has *bought* Ruth to be his wife in order to restore the dead to his rightful place in the community through the birth of the children of his widow. The witnesses to the scene accept their role as witnesses to the transaction and pray the blessing of fruitfulness on the couple—the fruitfulness of the foremothers of Israel.

With the marriage of Ruth and Boaz and the subsequent birth of a son—a "lad" to replace Naomi's dead sons, the story appears to be over. It has ended with a patriarchal burst, as Boaz the man redeems both Naomi and Ruth. Yet our narrator has one more surprise in store. As the women of the neighborhood proclaim the joy of the birth of the child, they turn our attention back to the heroine of our story. They say, "Your daughter-in-law who loves you, who is better for you than seven sons, has borne the lad." Not only are they right about Ruth, but they also have summarized the tale.

Ruth's love for her mother-in-law has been the central motivation from the beginning of the story. In act one Ruth threw her very life and future away for Naomi. In act two, Ruth risked her life again, going out to hostile fields to glean a meager living for Naomi. In act three, Ruth took risks again by going down to the threshing floor alone at midnight to ensure a future for herself and Naomi. There is no question that all of Ruth's actions have been motivated by her amazing love for Naomi. In this, she really is "better than seven sons." No matter how patriarchal the setting or the language of the story may be, Ruth shines through as a woman free of patriarchal strictures and male-dominant demands. Ruth's risk-taking, love, and devotion conquer all in this story. She found a world of emptiness, but her love moved it to a world of fullness both for herself and for Naomi, whom we last see playing with the grandfather of King David.

An empty world becomes a full world. This is a familiar story for Jews and Christians, who worship a God who time and again gazes upon an empty world and because of unfailing devotion and love sends prophets and apostles in order to move that world from emptiness to fullness. In act one of the story, Naomi asked God to be like Ruth by showing her the same kind of devotion and love that Ruth had shown to her and her dead son. "Be like Ruth, O God," she said. And God is just like Ruth. In fact, one way we might remember God is that God is a Moabite widow—perhaps even a Moabite widow who is deaf. Expand our ways of seeing, O God who is as Ruth to us, so that we may at last know that you are far more than our limited sight, far more than our limited loving, far more than our limited words.

> *Ruth 4:15 is a crucial line, so I use it as a way to point out that the actions of Ruth parallel the actions of God. My goal in this telling is to expand the ways in which God may be envisioned. My sermon offers two startling metaphors of God: deaf one and Moabite woman. I hope that these metaphors will break through the older stereotypes of God as an "old man in the sky" or other equally inadequate images. There can be no changes in a person's life without a change of metaphors. Before intellectual change is effected, old and inadequate metaphors must be challenged, discarded, and replaced by dynamic metaphors that enable change and growth to occur. Indeed, one of the greatest possibilities of narrative sermons is their potential to get at the metaphors of our lives, to challenge the things most basic to our personalities. To be able to see God as Ruth could be the beginning of a new journey of faith, a journey that includes partners in faith who until now have not been welcome on the trip—in this instance, women and the differently abled.*

SOME NARRATIVE NOTES TO THE SERMON

Plot

The book of Ruth is made up of eighty-five tightly plotted verses. It is replete with many plays on words, cross-references of scenes, and subtle characterizations. All of these details are delightful, but can hardly appear in any one sermon. Before any details may be employed, the plot must be sharply focused to avoid overemphasis on any one series of elements, regardless of how compelling they may be.

My sermon "God, the Moabite Widow" focuses on Ruth. In my reading, she is the one who motivates and energizes the plot. She risks her life three times, each time on behalf of her mother-in-law. In short, the dynamic sequential element of the story of Ruth centers on Ruth's own actions. This fact, however, does not necessarily rule out the possibility of focusing other narrative sermons based on the book of Ruth on Naomi or even Boaz, although a sermon focused on Boaz risks missing or seriously underplaying the obvious emphasis on the women in the story. One of the signs of a lively and engaged imagination in the act of preaching is the ability to emphasize other characters in the narrative to see how a new angle of vision can offer fresh insight into a text. Nonetheless, a careful reading of the plot of Ruth suggests that Ruth should be the centerpiece of a first narrative sermon based on this book.

Several other features of the plot add to the emphasis on Ruth.

1. The focus falls on the women very early, as each male is dead by verse 6.

2. Ruth's memorable speech (1:16-17) is uttered right after it has been made clear to Orpah and to the reader that any who follow after Naomi to Israel will be unwelcome and without future. Thus, the location of the speech is crucial for the plot and for the characterization of Ruth.

3. The location of Naomi's bitter speech (1:20-21) further isolates Ruth from Naomi, intensifies the hopelessness of Ruth's situation in Israel with Naomi, and strengthens the portrait of Ruth's resolution.

4. The note that they have arrived in Bethlehem at the "beginning of the barley harvest" (1:22) provides an important piece of chronological information that will find its significance at 2:23.

5. Although Ruth arrives at the field of Boaz serendipitously (Ruth 2:3), Boaz already knows a great deal about her when he first sees her working in his field. Indeed, he knows as much as

the reader knows and thus sees Ruth far more clearly than Naomi sees her. His speech to Ruth about what he knows (2:11-12), followed by his audaciously desperate attempts to make sure that Ruth will continue to return to his field for work (Ruth 2:14-16), suggests a speedy courtship and marriage. However, the apparently desperate Boaz slows the hunt considerably. We are told that Ruth continued to work in Boaz's fields "until the end of the barley and wheat harvests." This note, which closes the time-frame that began at the beginning of the barley harvest (Ruth 1:22), sets the actions of chapter 2 in a period of seven weeks. This long delay heightens the tension and leads to the astonishing plan of Naomi in chapter 3.

6. We do not know enough about Israelite sexual mores to feel the full weight of the plot of chapter 3. However, a careful reading of the actions of Boaz and Ruth as they converse on the threshing floor in the middle of the night suggests that the scene is fraught with danger. As I indicated in my notes within the body of the sermon, any telling of this scene should attempt to match the reticence and ambiguity of the original author. Although the word translated "legs" (or "feet") is sometimes used as a euphemism for genitals, this is no time for the preacher to offer explicit details. "She uncovered his legs" suggests the sexual ambiguity and retains the reticence of the text.

What is important for the plot in this scene is that another surprising twist is added when Boaz shockingly announces that some Israelite has prior rights to the property of which Ruth is a part. Thus, the lightness of the scene—its palpable joy—is sharply changed by this announcement. Any telling of the story should make clear this unexpected plot twist.

7. Haste characterizes Boaz as he rushes from the threshing floor to the gate of the city—the lower court of Israel. Naomi is right when she says, "He will not rest; he will settle the matter today" (3:18). And he does so with considerable cleverness. His first speech in the presence of the seated elders who are acting as jury for the case speaks only of property (4:3-4). "Mr. So-and-so" [1] eagerly decides to exercise his right of redemption. But Boaz adds, almost as an afterthought, that responsibility for Ruth comes with this property (4:3-4). As my sermon explains, the responsibility could prove to be a heavy one if the comparatively

youthful Ruth bears a son to inherit the property of his mother's first husband, thereby denying "So-and-so" any further proceeds from the property without removing his responsibility for the widow Ruth. Therefore, "So-and-so" changes his mind. Like Orpah before him, he takes the easy way, the less risky way.

8. Just as the plot dispenses with the males at the beginning of the story, so it does at the end of the story. Save the newborn son, only women conclude the tale. The women of the neighborhood announce to Naomi the astonishing conviction that Ruth is "to you more than seven sons." Though Naomi thought that she came back "empty" from the land of Moab and that the birth of the boy made her life full at last, the real truth of the story is that the woman Ruth is worth more than seven of the boys. Because seven is the number of completeness in this tradition, Ruth is, in fact, worth more than as many sons as one could count. With this claim, the narrator has commented on the plot in a surprising way. The birth of the child is not the climax or the point of this plot. Ruth, who is more than seven sons, is the climax and the point of the story. This claim throws into sharp relief all her actions from the very beginning of the story.

Character and Characterization

Again I will divide my brief comments on character and characterization into examples of the *actions* and the *speeches* of characters. I will restrict my discussion to those places that directly informed my sermon.

The Actions of Characters

Although there is no speech in the story until verse 8 of chapter 1, much happens before this point. There is famine, a family's move to a foreign land, the tragic death of the head of the family, two marriages, two more tragic deaths, the apparent end of the famine, and finally a return to the place of origin by the only remaining original traveler. But Naomi does not go alone; she is accompanied by her two Moabite daughters-in-law, Orpah and Ruth. All of these events lead to the first scene of confrontation between Naomi and the two younger women.

107

In quite lengthy and detailed speeches and in all of her actions, Naomi makes it very clear that she wants to be alone. Her first two speeches have the desired effect upon Orpah; Orpah weeps and kisses in farewell (1:14). The reader can hardly blame her actions. But we read that "Ruth clung to her." As I briefly noted in my comments within the sermon, the verb *clung* in Hebrew is a most powerfully intimate one (see Gen. 2:24, 34:3; I Kings 5:27; Josh. 23:12; II Sam. 20:2). Before Ruth utters a word, we learn a lesson about her powerful resolve in the face of rejection.

After Ruth's remarkable speech that seals her resolve, Naomi's silence suggests how unmoved and unchanged she is. This is made even clearer by Naomi's final speech of the chapter in which she declares herself completely empty, thus disavowing any recognition of the Moabite who has thrown her life away to accompany her mother-in-law into a strange land. So, Ruth's tenacious resolve, Naomi's unchangeable desire to be left alone, and Orpah's common sense are portrayed through simple actions and well-placed silences.

So it is with Boaz. All of his actions portray him as "a man of stature"[2] in the community—well-liked by his workers (2:4), and well-respected by his peers (the trial scene in 4:1-12). Yet, his one blemish appears to be his over-reticence with regard to Ruth. He fails to follow up on his overt attempts to keep her close to him (2:8-16) by allowing the budding relationship to languish for some seven weeks (2:23). It is his refusal to act that forces Naomi into the desperate action of chapter 3. Nevertheless, when Boaz finally is faced directly with his responsibility as "near redeemer" by Ruth herself, he acts honorably and even cleverly at the trial to gain Ruth as his bride.

Three statements can be made about the actions of Ruth. First, in all actions she takes great personal risk: on the Bethlehem road, in the foreign field, and on the threshing floor. Second, in all actions she thinks first of her mother-in-law: on the Bethlehem road, in the foreign field (note especially that the food that she did not eat she gave to Naomi—2:18), and on the threshing floor (note Ruth's lie to Naomi about the grain given to her by Boaz—3:17).

Third, in all actions she is in full control: on the Bethlehem road, in her decision to go to the foreign field, and even on the threshing floor. Though Naomi told her that the man would "tell you what do do" (3:4), it is Ruth who tells *him* what to do (3:9). Boaz himself tells her that he "will do for you all that you ask" (3:11).

The narrator demonstrates a fine use of contrast in the story that also contributes to characterization. When we compare Orpah to Ruth, we find, through the actions of the former, a sensible woman who responds to the arguments of Naomi by going home—a perfectly logical thing to do. Yet as a result of this logic, the empty world of the widows remains empty. It is only the quite illogical risks of Ruth that bring about the fullness of the story's conclusion. Likewise, when we compare Boaz to "Mr. So-and-so," the latter has a logical reaction to the economic problem represented by the young widow Ruth. He washes his hands of the whole deal, as any shrewd business person would have done. Boaz, in contrast, does the honorable thing by marrying the needy widow, thus preserving the line of her deceased husband. In offering these contrasts, the narrator highlights the virtues of Ruth and Boaz, the two on whom the reader is to focus attention.

The Speeches of Characters

By focusing attention on the first speech of two of the main characters, I will examine how the narrator has used speech to intensify characterization.

First let us examine Naomi's first speech, which is found in two related parts in Ruth 1:8-13.

> (8) Go! Return! Each one to the house of her mother. May Yahweh act devotedly with you in the same way that you have acted devotedly with the dead and with me. (9) May Yahweh give to you in order that you find rest, each of you in the house of her husband. (Author's translation)

Naomi begins her speech with two sharp imperative verbs. Thus the central purpose of the speech is made very clear: Naomi does not want Orpah and Ruth to accompany her to Israel. No reason is suggested for this desire, but it is clear that Naomi wants no company on this trip. She goes on to praise the women's actions with their dead husbands and with her, and she expresses her hope that the God of Israel will act toward them as devotedly as they have acted. However she concludes her argument by insisting that the only place Yahweh might so act on their behalf is in Moab—first in the "house of your mother" and finally in "the house of your husband." Actually, Naomi does not argue at all; she merely paints a glowing picture of the wonderful options in Moab for two widowed Moabites. By implication, such options will not be available in Judah. Her entire speech, then, is designed to do one thing: get rid of the two Moabites. Naomi's kiss of verse 9 is a kiss of farewell.

But Naomi's plan does not work; the women insist that they "will return with you to your people." The women shift the discussion from the possible hope in Moab to the prospects of life with the people of Naomi. So, Naomi tells a story about life back in Israel.

> (11) Return, my daughters! Why will you go with me? Have I still sons in my womb that they might become your husbands? (12) Turn back, my daughters! Go your way! Surely, I am too old to have a husband. If I should say, "There is hope for me! Why, I could have a husband this night and bear sons," (13) for them would you wait until they grew up? For them would you restrain yourselves, not getting a husband? No, my daughters, it is far more bitter for me than for you! Surely, the hand of Yahweh has gone against me!

In Naomi's question "Why will you go with me?" is a tone of absurdity. The implication is that only a fool would make such a choice. Naomi then offers to Orpah and Ruth the problem they face in Judah as she interpets the working of the tradition of levirate marriage.[3] Naomi is too old to have any more sons; her womb is closed. In a sarcastic fantasy, she describes what would have to happen for the two Moabites to have any real hope among the people of Israel: immediate marriage for Naomi, to a man (*do you see any?*), immediate conception (*I just told you my womb is empty!*), a minimal fifteen-year wait for the boy (*if it is a boy*) to grow up. Naomi is implying, "By then the two of *you* would be old! You should not wait for such an impossibility."

Naomi caps her fantasy with the phrase "No, my daughters; it is far more bitter for me than for you." Her use of the word *bitter* indicates the tone of the previous speech and possibly suggests that Naomi's real concern here is not for the well-being of her daughters-in-law, at least not *only* for their well-being. Naomi, a deeply embittered and lonely widow, concludes by placing blame for her condition on the one she knows to be the cause of all. "The hand of Yahweh has gone forth against me."

When we add this speech to the actions of Naomi previously, we see an angry, bitter, and caustic woman who is strained to the breaking point by the deaths she has endured. The narrator does not judge her or blame her; the narrator merely characterizes her in actions and speech and thus adds her to the ongoing dynamic of the plot. As the preacher searches for ways to bring Naomi's character to life in the telling, he or she will find abundant clues for a modern portrayal.

Similarly, Ruth's great speech in the first chapter provides a fitting characterization of this remarkable woman.

> (16) Do not force me to abandon you, to return from following you. Surely, wherever you go, I will go, and wherever you lodge, I will lodge. Your people will be my people, your God, my God. (17) Wherever you die, I will die, and there I will be buried. Thus may Yahweh do to me, and even more, if death divides me from you!

Naomi has just convinced Orpah to return to Moab, but Ruth still clings to her. One can almost hear Naomi say, "What is wrong with you, anyway?" The reader is just as astonished as Naomi; why *is* Ruth acting and talking like this? The narrator draws Ruth's character with care in this speech.

Ruth reveals who she is early in her speech. "Do not force me to abandon you," she says. To leave Naomi at this point in her life would be nothing less than abandonment. The Naomi revealed to us and to Ruth in the preceding speech is bitter and angry. Once full of hope and promise, she is now empty of both. Ruth will not abandon one such as that. The remainder of Ruth's speech—with its unforgettable rhetorical flourishes that move through following, lodging, worshiping, and dying together—illustrates Ruth's unshakable refusal to abandon her mother-in-law. It is an instance of devotion, pure and simple—but by no means less powerful for its simplicity and purity. Ruth ends her assertion of absolute devotion with an oath in the name of Yahweh, the only time that divine name is found on her lips in the entire story. By so speaking, she intends to convince Naomi, and us, of her complete sincerity.

As in the case of Naomi, the narrator has begun a careful characterization of Ruth through action and speech. In the face of rejection, Ruth refuses to abandon Naomi; she clings to her in devotion. Likewise, in her first speech, that devotion is given memorable verbal expression. No reader can be unaware of the remarkable woman whose story is about to unfold. The narrative preacher may use these findings of action and speech as building blocks toward the construction of the narrative sermon. The clues to effective construction are to be found in the narrative itself.

The Speeches' Effects on Plot

The first speeches of Naomi and Ruth play an important role in the plot of the narrative. As a result of these speeches, several questions are raised in the mind of the reader—questions related to the motives of the characters. For example, why is Naomi so anxious to be alone? Is she just bitter (as I suggested by my reading), or is she also uncomfortable around these foreigners, these Moabites?[4] This ambiguity of motive is a result of what has been called "gaps" in the art of biblical narration.[5] The narrators of the Bible are reticent in making clear why a character is acting and speaking as she or he is. Much of the pleasure of reading the Bible's narratives comes from these gaps. The reader's attempts to close these gaps urge her or him along the plot of the narrative.

For example, can we be certain that Ruth's primary motive for following Naomi is pure devotion? Might further actions and speeches reveal other motives, such as the desire for security or the fear of isolation? Such conclusions can be made only after carefully reading subsequent actions and speeches in the light of actions and speeches already examined. Perhaps the key to the plot of the biblical narrative is paying attention to the gaps in the narrative and to various clues given by the narrator as possible ways to close the gaps. I would conclude, for example, that whatever gap is created for Ruth's motives is closed in Ruth 4:15 when the women of the neighborhood announce to Naomi what *all* of Ruth's actions and speeches have suggested from the beginning: that she "loves" her mother-in-law. This is the only time in the story that the word *love* is used—a fact that highlights its truth.

The narrative preacher must examine with considerable care the actions and speeches of the characters of the stories and keep a fully open mind concerning the possibly shifting motivations for those actions and speeches. Such careful attention will prove valuable in the lively construction of a narrative sermon that hopes to capture something of the tone and flavor of the original narrative.

Point of View

A modern analogy is the best way to describe the use of point of view in the narration of Ruth. This narrator writes in much the same way that you and I are "allowed" to watch television. Television has what appears to be full control over its viewers. That is, we are able to see only what the camera will allow us to see. As much as we might like to see the reactions on the faces of the reporters listening to the president's remarks at a press conference, we seldom are given that privilege by the camera. We are thus in part manipulated by the images we are allowed to see. Of course, this benign example becomes more dangerous when the only images we receive are slanted or biased in such a way to give us a completely false view of an event. In any case, we are under the control of the camera for what we are able to see.

The same is true in the narrative of Ruth. The style is quite cinematic.

(1) Now Naomi had a relative through her husband, a man of substance, from the family of Elimelech, named Boaz. (2) Ruth said to her mother-in-law, to Naomi, "I will go to the field, and I will glean among the ears of grain after the one in whose eyes I find favor." She said to her, "Go, my daughter." (3) So she went out, came, and gleaned in the field after the harvesters.

Boaz is introduced to us in verse 1 as Naomi's relative from the family of her dead husband, Elimelech. He also is described as a man of "substance," one with stature in the community. It is little more than a still picture of Boaz, but it is enough to stimulate our thoughts about his possible role in the plot of the story. The narrator's camera then quickly moves us to the place where Ruth and Naomi are living, just in time to hear Ruth say to Naomi that she is about to go to work—to glean in a strange and foreign field. Naomi acquiesces with a muttered pleasantry. Just as quickly, Ruth goes to the field to pick up the meager fare of a foreign gleaner. The narrator's camera then moves us through three scenes very rapidly. By juxtaposing the scenes so closely, the narrator has energized the plot. The snapshot of Boaz brings into the story precisely what Naomi had ruled impossible in chapter 1: a possible marriage for one of the widows. The brief scene of Ruth leaving the house to glean in an unknown field brings the possibility that somehow she will end up in the place where Boaz is, and that is precisely what happens.

The narrative preacher can learn from this marvelous economy of words and scenes how little it takes to set a mood clearly and expansively. Likewise, by noting the way that the narrator directs the attentions of the reader by the use of point of view, the narrative preacher can learn to avoid emphasizing elements of the text that are not emphasized by the narrator.

Clues Toward the Narrative Sermon

My reading of the narrative of Ruth found Ruth to be the center of the tale. Her consistent portrayal as a woman who risks her reputation and her very life for her mother-in-law forms the point around which the other characters circle. Just as Naomi is saved by Ruth, so Boaz plays his role of redeemer/next-of-kin only after being prompted by Ruth on the threshing floor. Ruth, therefore, became the logical focus for my narrative sermon.

Because Ruth is a very complex story, the wonderful details provided by a close reading could easily obscure a clear goal for a narrative sermon. This is why I more narrowly focused my attention on the times in the story when the actions of Ruth were compared to the actions of God. Naomi raises this idea first in Ruth 1:8 and then connects Ruth's devotion to the kind of devotion that Yahweh can show in Ruth 2:20. Boaz also recognizes Ruth's devotion to Naomi (2:11-12), and later applauds her devotion to him because she has chosen him over younger and presumably more desirable men (3:10). Ruth's actions of devotion throughout the story clearly are reminiscent of the actions of Yahweh. Ruth's world was a world of emptiness characterized by death—no food, no future. Through her devoted risks, she changes that world from emptiness to fullness. The tale ends with plenty of food, a future culminating in David the king, and new life for Naomi—the formerly barren and bitter one. Ruth's devotion to those around her mirrors God's devotion to the world God created.

I chose a frame narrative style to point the sermon from the very beginning to the concern of Ruth as the surprising revealer of God, hence my title, "God, the Moabite Widow." A frame helps the hearer to center more directly and more quickly on my concern for this narrative, thereby avoiding the dangers of losing the sermon's central goal in the story itself.

As in my pure narrative in chapter 4, I began with the end—the goal of my telling. I composed the sermon toward that end, and I provide clues along the way so that the goal is never too far from the surface of the story. I find this to be one of the chief dangers of narrative preaching: the goal of the telling will disappear under the overt pleasure of the telling itself. The narrative preacher, like any preacher, must keep the goal of the telling in mind as the sermon is composed and delivered. Once the goal is articulated—in this case, Ruth is the mirror of God—then the story can be told with that goal guiding the telling. Any details that may be uncovered in the reading of the story but that do not serve the goal should be discarded, however painful that might be.

AFTERWORD

> How have you left the ancient love
> That bards of old enjoyed in you!
> The languid strings do scarcely move!
> The sound is forced, the notes are few![1]

This final stanza from William Blake's poem "To the Muses" imaginatively captures, in part, the reason for the existence of this book. The nine Muses of Greek mythology were those creatures who offered the possibility or withheld the possibility of creative, artistic expression. When the muses were generous with the gifts of poetic expression, great works of art were produced; when the muses hid their faces, no amount of sweaty labor could bring forth art worthy of the name. Blake calls on the muses of the past again to enliven an eighteenth century art, characterized as possessing "languid strings, forced sounds, and few notes."

I do not intend to join the chorus of lamentation that is being raised over the supposed demise, or the terminal illness, or at least the virulent sickness of the art of preaching as practiced in our time. Nor do I intend to claim that narrative preaching is the only effective way to preach in our media-conscious culture. I do believe that effective preaching is being done in churches and synagogues throughout the world, much of which is being done in non-narrative modes.

Yet, like Blake, I must say that much of the preaching I hear unfortunately is often characterized by "languid strings, forced sounds, and few notes." It remains pallid, uninteresting, uninspired, and uninspiring. This book is a modest attempt to intro-

116

duce another way to present the message of God's love and will for relationship with freshness and power. Such a method will not rescue a failed preaching ministry, nor will it bring a successful preacher down. What it will do is enthuse preachers to experiment with a new mode of presentation and offer them specific ways to attempt the new mode as well as specific theological suggestions for why one should try it in the first place.

The ministry of preaching is alive in the land and often in many places is also well. Many of you who are reading this book are already preaching effectively. You are preaching effectively to real congregations who live in real life circumstances. Those of us who are not currently privileged to serve a congregation of regular worshipers cannot do the effective pulpit ministry that you can do. This is true because great preaching cannot be done without a deep understanding of those who hear. Only church pastors have the opportunity to know—really *know*—those who hear their sermons. Therefore, I dedicate this modest book to you—you who preach to those you know. May your strings vibrate with the power of God's Spirit, may your sounds be infused with the voice of God, and may your notes be tuneful and clear. I hope that this book has reenergized you for the great ministry of preaching which has been given to you by God, who is the final narrator of us all.

NOTES

INTRODUCTION

1. I have chosen to use the name "Hebrew Bible" for the collection of works traditionally called the Old Testament by Christians. The term *Old Testament* is, of course, a term dependent upon the *New Testament*, both terms being rooted in the concept of the new and old covenants in Jeremiah 31:31-34. For Christians there are indeed important ways in which the Hebrew Bible is certainly old. Yet for Jewish people, the term *Old Testament* is at best displeasing, implying something inferior and secondary. And the designation has played no small part in the loss of those materials from the churches of the late twentieth century. After all, if we have something new, why should we be seriously concerned with something old? I trust the term *Hebrew Bible* will prove understandable to Christians, part of whose Holy Scripture it is, as well as inviting to Jewish sisters and brothers whose Holy Scripture it also is, albeit in obviously different ways.
2. John Bright, *The Authority of the Old Testament* (Nashville: Abingdon, 1967) p. 151.
3. Ibid., p. 92.
4. See John C. Holbert, " 'Deliverance Belongs to Yahweh!': Satire in the Book of Jonah," *Journal for Study of the Old Testament* 21 (1981): 59-81.
5. Thomas G. Long, *Preaching and the Literary Forms of the Bible* (Philadelphia: Fortress, 1989), p. 29.
6. Elizabeth Achtemeier, *The Old Testament and the Proclamation of the Gospel* (Philadelphia: Westminster, 1973), p. 142.
7. Foster R. McCurley, Jr., *Proclaiming the Promise* (Philadelphia: Fortress, 1974), p. 39; Donald E. Gowan, *Reclaiming the Old Testament for the Christian Pulpit* (Atlanta: John Knox, 1980), p. 4.
8. Elizabeth Achtemeier, *Preaching from the Old Testament* (Louisville:

Westminster/John Knox, 1989).
9. Gowan, *Reclaiming the Old Testament*, p. 13.
10. Ibid., p. 56.
11. Achtemeier, *The Old Testament*, pp. 20-21.
12. Achtemeier, *Preaching from the Old Testament*, pp. 39-44.
13. See John C. Holbert, "Joseph and the Surprising Choice of God," *Perkins Journal*, (Summer 1985): 33-42.
14. Achtemeir, *Preaching from the Old Testament*, p. 61.
15. Ibid., p. 63.
16. Ibid., p. 61.
17. Ibid., pp. 16-19.
18. Long, *Preaching and the Literary Forms*, pp. 66-86.

1. A THEOLOGICAL REFLECTION ON NARRATIVE

1. Elie Wiesel, *The Gates of the Forest* (New York: Avon Books, 1967), p. 10.
2. Fred B. Craddock, *Preaching* (Nashville: Abingdon, 1985), p. 65.
3. "Doctrinal Standards and our Theological Task," part 2 of *The Book of Discipline of the United Methodist Church* (Nashville: The United Methodist Publishing House, 1988), p. 81.
4. Ibid., p. 82.
5. Ibid.
6. Ibid., pp. 82-83.
7. Gerhard von Rad, *Genesis, a Commentary*, 2nd ed. (Philadelphia: Westminster, 1971), p. 152.
8. Michael Goldberg, *Jews and Christians* (Nashville: Abingdon, 1985), p. 13.
9. Quoted in Wiesel, *The Gates of the Forest*, epigram page.
10. I am grateful to Walter Brueggemann for the origin of this insight about the loss of the story. See his *Israel's Praise* (Philadelphia: Fortress, 1988), pp. 107-8. I have used the idea for very different purposes than those suggested by Brueggemann.
11. Johann Baptist Metz, *Faith in History and Society: Toward a Practical Fundamental Theology* (New York: Crossroad, 1980), p. 212.
12. Ibid.
13. Sallie TeSelle, *Speaking in Parables* (Philadelphia: Fortress, 1975), p. 32. TeSelle now writes under the name of Sallie McFague.
14. Ibid., p. 13.
15. Ibid., p. 15.
16. The reader is referred to the following works as examples of literary-critical analyses of parables: Dan Otto Via, Jr., *The Parables* (Philadelphia: Fortress, 1967); John Dominic Crossan, *In Parables* (New York: Harper & Row, 1973); James Breech, *The Silence of Jesus* (Philadelphia:

Fortress, 1983); Madeleine Boucher, *The Mysterious Parable* (Washington, D.C.: The Catholic Biblical Association of America, 1977); Mary Ann Tolbert, *Perspectives on the Parables* (Philadelphia: Fortress, 1979).

17. Stephen Crites, "Angels We Have Heard," in James B. Wiggens, ed. *Religion as Story* (New York: Harper & Row, 1975), pp. 23-63.

18. Ibid., p. 31.

19. Stephen Crites, "The Narrative Quality of Experience," *Journal of The American Academy of Religion* 39 (September 1971), pp. 291-311.

20. Ibid., p. 295.

21. Ibid.

22. Ibid.

23. Ibid., p. 296.

24. Crites, "Angels We Have Heard," p. 57 n. 4.

25. See the fictional experiments of Robbe-Grillet or Samuel Beckett.

26. Crites, "The Narrative Quality of Experience," p. 297.

27. Ibid.

28. Ibid., p. 303.

29. Ibid., p. 305.

30. Ibid., p. 307.

2. NARRATIVE PREACHING

1. Don M. Wardlaw, ed., *Preaching Biblically* (Philadelphia: Westminster, 1983), pp. 12-14.

2. Fred B. Craddock, *As One Without Authority* (Nashville: Abingdon, 1971), pp. 143-44.

3. Henry H. Mitchell, *The Recovery of Preaching* (New York: Harper & Row, 1977), pp. 25-26.

4. Richard L. Eslinger, *A New Hearing* (Nashville: Abingdon, 1987), p. 160.

5. Ibid.

6. Because I am a white male Protestant, I necessarily base my observations on an experience most often characterized by those sociological facts. Nearly every book on the subject of preaching suggests that the African-American preaching experience is a significant exception to the problems being addressed. My own familiarity with African-American preaching tells me that this is correct. However, not all African-American preachers whom I have heard preach escape the discursive mode completely.

7. John A. Broadus, *On the Preparation and Delivery of Sermons*, 4th ed. rev. by Vernon L. Stanfield (New York: Harper & Row, 1979), p. 132.

8. H. Grady Davis, *Design for Preaching* (Philadelphia: Fortress, 1958), p. 157.

9. Ibid., p. 5.

10. Ibid., p. 162.
11. James W. Cox, *Preaching* (San Francisco: Harper & Row, 1985), p. 161.
12. F. Dean Lueking, *Preaching* (Waco, Texas: Word, 1985), p. 96.
13. Frederick Buechner, *Telling the Truth* (New York: Harper & Row, 1977), p. 91.
14. Fred Craddock, *Overhearing the Gospel* (Nashville: Abingdon, 1978), p. 137.
15. Mitchell, *The Recovery of Preaching*, pp. 155-56.
16. Richard A. Jensen, *Telling the Story* (Minneapolis: Augsburg, 1980), p. 129; *How to Preach a Parable* by Eugene Lowry (Nashville: Abingdon, 1989) defines narrative preaching quite differently. For Lowry, any sermon that has a narrative shape, that moves from crisis to reversal to resolution, is a narrative sermon, regardless of its content. My definition is obviously much more restricted.
17. Sally Fitzgerald, ed. *The Habit of Being* (New York: Random House, 1979), p. 79.
18. Amos N. Wilder, *Early Christian Rhetoric* (Cambridge: Harvard University Press, 1964) pp. 126-27.
19. Craddock, *Overhearing the Gospel*, p. 82.
20. Jensen, *Telling the Story*, p. 145.
21. Richard Lischer, "The Limits of Story," *Interpretation* 38 (January 1984): 26-38.
22. Ibid., p. 27.
23. Ibid., p. 31.
24. Ibid., p. 32.
25. Ibid., p. 35.
26. Ibid.
27. These two terms, *chording* and *whooping*, are attempts to describe those occasions in some African-American sermons where the preacher breaks into chant-like song or repeated rhythmic phrases.
28. Ronald E. Sleeth, *God's Word & Our Words* (Atlanta: John Knox, 1986), p. 98.
29. Helps for the preacher's imagination may be found in Paul Scott Wilson, *Imagination of the Heart* (Nashville: Abingdon, 1988), and Thomas H. Troeger, *Imagining the Sermon* (Nashville: Abingdon, 1990).

3. READING THE BIBLE'S NARRATIVE

1. Walter Wink, *The Bible in Human Transformation* (Philadelphia: Fortress, 1973), p. 1.
2. Ibid.
3. Ibid., p. 2.

4. Ibid.
5. John Barton, *Reading the Old Testament* (Philadelphia: Westminster, 1984), p. 201.
6. Ibid., p. 43.
7. Klaus Koch, *The Growth of Biblical Tradition* (New York: Scribner's, 1969), p. 57.
8. Barton, *Reading the Old Testament*, p. 45.
9. von Rad, *Genesis*, pp. 143-45.
10. T. S. Eliot, *The Use of Poetry and the Use of Criticism* (Cambridge: Harvard University Press, 1933), p. 153.
11. Meir Sternberg, *The Poetics of Biblical Narrative* (Bloomington: Indiana University Press, 1985), p. 68.
12. James L. Kugel, *The Idea of Biblical Poetry* (New Haven: Yale University Press, 1981), p. 303.
13. Kenneth R. R. Gros Louis, *Literary Interpretations of Biblical Narratives*, vol. II (Nashville: Abingdon, 1982), p. 16.
14. For a classic statement of this distinction, see E. D. Hirsch, *Validity in Interpretation* (New Haven: Yale University Press, 1967), especially pp. 1-23.
15. Robert Scholes and Robert Kellogg, *The Nature of Narrative* (London: Oxford University Press, 1966), p. 207.
16. Ibid., p. 208.
17. Wayne Booth, *The Rhetoric of Fiction* (Chicago: University of Chicago Press, 1961), p. 126.
18. John C. Holbert, "Joseph and the Surprising Choice of God," *Perkins Journal* (Summer 1985): 33-42.
19. Henry James, "The Art of Fiction," quoted in Scholes and Kellogg, *The Nature of Narrative*, p. 160.
20. Adele Berlin, *Poetics and Interpretation of Biblical Narrative* (Sheffield, England: Almond Press, 1983), p. 23.
21. Ibid., p. 30.
22. Ibid., p. 31.
23. Though many translations add the phrase "to the Hebrews" to Exod. 1:22, the Hebrew text says: "Every son that is born."
24. Robert Alter, *The Art of Biblical Narrative* (New York: Basic Books, 1981), p. 81.
25. Ibid.
26. Scholes and Kellogg, *The Nature of Narrative*, p. 166.
27. Berlin, *Poetics*, pp. 40-41.
28. Scholes and Kellogg, *The Nature of Narrative*, p. 240.
29. Ibid., p. 241.
30. See Berlin, *Poetics*, pp. 79-82 for further discussion of these two reports.

4. A PURE NARRATIVE SERMON

1. Eric Auerbach, *Mimesis,* Willard R. Trask, trans. (Princeton, N. J.: Princeton University Press, 1953), pp. 10, 12.
2. John Skinner, *Genesis* (Edinburgh: T & T Clark, 1930), p. 329.
3. Kenneth R. R. Gros Louis, ed., *Literary Interpretations of Biblical Narratives,* vol. II (Nashville: Abingdon, 1982), pp. 79-80.
4. Everett Fox, *In the Beginning* (New York: Schocken, 1983), p. 83.
5. For examples of failed tests, see Exod. 15:25, 16:4, 20:20, and Deut. 8:2.
6. Fox, *In the Beginning,* p. 83.

5. A FRAME NARRATIVE SERMON

1. See Edward Campbell, Jr., *Ruth* (Garden City, N. Y.: Doubleday, 1975), pp. 141-43, for the rationale of this translation.
2. Ibid., p. 90. Campbell suggests "man of substance." His discussion presents the problems of translation.
3. Roland de Vaux, *Ancient Israel,* vol. 1 (New York: McGraw-Hill, 1965), pp. 37-40.
4. Danna Nolan Fewell and David M. Gunn, " 'A Son Is Born to Naomi!': Literary Allusions and Interpretation in the Book of Ruth," *Journal for the Study of the Old Testament,* 40 (1988): 99-108.
5. See Meir Sternberg, *The Poetics of Biblical Narrative* (Bloomington: Indiana University Press, 1985), especially chapter 6, pp. 186-229.

AFTERWORD

1. William Blake, "To the Muses," 1783. See M. H. Abrams, general ed., *The Norton Anthology of English Literature* (New York: W. W. Norton, 1962), p. 922.

SELECTED BIBLIOGRAPHY

1. THEOLOGY AND NARRATIVE

Crites, Stephen. "The Narrative Quality of Experience." *Journal of the American Academy of Religion* 39 (September 1971): 291-311.

———. "Angels We Have Heard." In *Religion as Story*, edited by James B. Wiggins. New York: Harper & Row, 1964.

Crossan, John Dominic. *The Dark Interval*. Niles, Ill.: Argus, 1975.

Damrosch, David. *The Narrative Covenant*. San Francisco: Harper & Row, 1987.

Ellingsen, Mark. *The Integrity of Biblical Narrative*. Minneapolis: Augsburg, 1990.

Goldberg, Michael. *Theology and Narrative*. Nashville: Abingdon, 1981.

Hauerwas, Stanley. *Truthfulness and Tragedy*. Notre Dame, Ind.: University of Notre Dame Press, 1977.

———. *A Community of Character*. Notre Dame, Ind.: University of Notre Dame Press, 1981.

McFague, Sallie. *Metaphorical Theology*. Philadelphia: Fortress, 1982.

Metz, Johann Baptist. *Faith in History and Society: Toward a Practical Fundamental Theology*. New York: Crossroad, 1980.

Stroup, George W. *The Promise of Narrative Theology*. Atlanta: John Knox, 1981.

TeSelle, Sallie. *Speaking in Parables*. Philadelphia: Fortress, 1975.

Tracy, David. *Blessed Rage for Order*. Minneapolis: Seabury, 1975.

———. *The Analogical Question*. New York: Crossroad, 1981.

———. *Plurality and Ambiguity*. San Francisco: Harper & Row, 1987.

Wicker, Brian. *The Story-Shaped World*. Notre Dame, Ind.: Universtiy of Notre Dame Press, 1975.

Wiggens, James B., ed. *Religion as Story*. New York: Harper & Row, 1975.

2. NARRATIVE PREACHING

Bausch, William J. *Storytelling: Imagination and Faith.* Mystic, Conn.: Twenty-Third Publications, 1984.

Boomershine, Thomas E. *Story Journey.* Nashville: Abingdon, 1988.

Buechner, Fredrick. *Telling the Truth.* New York: Harper & Row, 1977.

Chatfield, Donald F. *Dinner with Jesus.* Grand Rapids: Zondervan, 1988.

Craddock, Fred B. *As One Without Authority.* Nashville: Abingdon, 1971.

————. *Overhearing the Gospel.* Nashville: Abingdon, 1978.

Eslinger, Richard L. *A New Hearing.* Nashville: Abingdon, 1987.

Gowan, Donald E. *Reclaiming the Old Testament for the Christian Pulpit.* Atlanta: John Knox, 1980.

Jensen, Richard A. *Telling the Story.* Minneapolis: Augsburg, 1980.

Long, Thomas G. *Preaching and the Literary Forms of the Bible.* Philadelphia: Fortress, 1989.

Lowry, Eugene L. *The Homiletical Plot.* Atlanta: John Knox, 1980.

————. *Doing Time in the Pulpit.* Nashville: Abingdon, 1985.

————. *How to Preach a Parable.* Nashville: Abingdon, 1989.

Markquart, Edward F. *Quest for Better Preaching.* Minneapolis: Augsburg, 1985.

Mitchell, Henry H. *The Recovery of Preaching.* New York: Harper & Row, 1977.

O'Day, Gail R. *The Word Disclosed.* St. Louis: CBP, 1987.

Robinson, Wayne Bradley, Ed. *Journeys Toward Narrative Preaching.* New York: Pilgrim, 1990.

Salmon, Bruce C. *Storytelling as Preaching.* Nashville: Broadman, 1989.

Sanders, James, A. *God Has a Story Too.* Philadelphia: Fortress, 1979.

Steimle, Edmund A., Morris J. Niedenthal and Charles L. Rice. *Preaching the Story.* Philadelphia: Fortress, 1980.

Wagley, Laurence A. *Preaching with the Small Congregation.* Nashville: Abingdon, 1989.

Wardlaw, Don M. *Preaching Biblically.* Philadelphia: Westminster, 1983.

White, Richard C. *Biblical Preaching.* St. Louis: CBP, 1988.

3. BIBLICAL NARRATIVE

Alonso-Schökel, Luis. *A Manual of Hebrew Poetics.* Rome: Pontifical Biblical Institute, 1988.

Alter, Robert. *The Art of Biblical Narrative.* New York: Basic Books, 1981.

Auerbach, Erich. *Mimesis.* Translated by Willard R. Trask. Princeton, N. J.: Princeton University Press, 1953.

Bal, Mieke. *Lethal Love.* Bloomington: Indiana University Press, 1987.

Bar-Efrat, Shimon. *Narrative Art in the Bible.* Sheffield, England: Almond Press, 1989.

Barton, John. *Reading the Old Testament.* Philadelphia: Westminster, 1984.

Berlin, Adele. *Poetics and Interpretation of Biblical Narrative.* Sheffield, England: Almond Press, 1983.

Booth, Wayne C. *The Rhetoric of Fiction.* Chicago: University of Chicago Press, 1961.

———. *The Rhetoric of Irony.* Chicago: University of Chicago Press, 1974.

———. *The Company We Keep.* Berkeley: University of California Press, 1988.

Buss, Martin J., ed. *Encounter with the Text.* Philadelphia: Fortress, 1979.

Caird, G. B. *The Language and Imagery of the Bible.* Philadelphia: Westminster, 1980.

Clines, David J. A., David M. Gunn and Alan J. Hauser, eds. *Art and Meaning: Rhetoric in Biblical Literature.* Sheffield, England: Journal for the Study of the Old Testament, 1982.

Culley, Robert C. *Studies in the Structure of Hebrew Narrative.* Philadelphia: Fortress, 1976.

Eslinger, Lyle M. *Kingship of God in Crisis.* Sheffield, England: Almond Press, 1985.

Fishbane, Michael. *Text and Texture.* New York: Schocken, 1979.

Frei, Hans. *The Eclipse of Biblical Narrative.* New Haven: Yale University Press, 1974.

Frye, Northrup. *The Anatomy of Criticism.* Princeton, N. J.: Princeton University Press, 1957.

———*The Great Code.* New York: Harcourt, Brace, Jovanovich, 1982.

Good, Edwin M. *Irony in the Old Testament.* Philadelphia: Westminster, 1965.

Greidanus, Sidney. *The Modern Preacher and the Ancient Text.* Grand Rapids: Eerdmans, 1988.

Gros Louis, Kenneth R. R., ed. *Literary Interpretations of Biblical Narratives.* 2 vols. Nashville: Abingdon, 1974, 1982.

Gunn, David M. *The Story of King David.* Sheffield, England: Journal for the Study of the Old Testament, 1978.

———. *The Fate of King Saul.* Sheffield, England: Journal for the Study of the Old Testament, 1980.

Hirsch, E. D., Jr., *Validity in Interpretation.* New Haven: Yale University Press, 1967.

Kermode, Frank. *The Sense of an Ending.* London: Oxford University Press, 1966.

———. *The Genesis of Secrecy.* Cambridge: Harvard University Press, 1979.

Long, Burke O., ed. *Images of God and Man.* Sheffield, England: Almond Press, 1981.

McKnight, Edgar V. *Post-Modern Use of the Bible.* Nashville: Abingdon, 1988.

Miscall, Peter D. *The Workings of Old Testament Narrative.* Philadlephia: Fortress, 1983.

————. *I Samuel: A Literary Reading.* Bloomington: Indiana University Press, 1986.

Polzin, Robert M. *Biblical Structuralism.* Philadelphia: Fortress, 1977.

————. *Moses and the Deuteronomist.* New York: Seabury, 1980.

————. *Samuel and the Deuteronomist.* San Francisco: Harper & Row, 1989.

Polzin, Robert M. and Eugene Rothman, eds. *The Biblical Mosiac.* Philadelphia: Fortress, 1982.

Robertson, David. *The Old Testament and the Literary Critic.* Philadelphia: Fortress, 1977.

Rosenberg, Joel. *King and Kin.* Bloomington: Indiana University Press, 1986.

Scholes, Robert and Robert Kellogg. *The Nature of Narrative.* London: Oxford University Press, 1966.

Sternberg, Meir. *The Poetics of Biblical Narrative.* Bloomington: Indiana University Press, 1985.

Wilder, Amos N. *Early Christian Rhetoric.* New York: Harper & Row, 1964.

4. OTHER BOOKS CONSULTED

Achtemeir, Elizabeth. *The Old Testament and the Proclamation of the Gospel.* Philadelphia: Westminster, 1973.

————. *Preaching as Theology and Art.* Nashville: Abingdon, 1984.

————. *Preaching from the Old Testament.* Louisville: Westminster/John Knox, 1989.

Alter, Robert and Frank Kermode, eds. *The Literary Guide to the Bible.* Cambridge: Harvard University Press, 1987.

Beardslee, William. *Biblical Preaching on the Death of Jesus.* Nashville: Abingdon, 1989.

Broadus, John A. *On the Preparation and Delivery of Sermons.* Revised by Vernon L. Stanfield. San Francisco: Harper & Row, 1979.

Brueggeman, Walter, *Finally Comes the Poet.* Minneapolis: Fortress, 1989.

————. *Israel's Praise.* Philadelphia: Fortress, 1988.

Burke, John, O. P., ed. *A New Look at Preaching.* Wilmington, Del.: Michael Glazier, 1983.

Buttrick, David. *Homiletic.* Philadelphia: Fortress, 1987.

Cox, James W. *Preaching.* San Francisco: Harper & Row, 1985.

Craddock, Fred B. *Preaching.* Nashville: Abingdon, 1985.

Davis, H. Grady. *Design for Preaching.* Philadelphia: Fortress, 1958.

Jones, Ilion T. *Principles and Practice of Preaching.* Nashville: Abingdon, 1956.

Josipovici, Gabriel. *The Book of God.* New Haven: Yale University Press, 1988.

Kennel, LeRoy E. *Preaching as Shared Story.* Dubuque, Iowa: Kendall/ Hunt, 1987.

Morgan, Peter M. *Story Weaving.* St. Louis: CBP, 1986.

Sleeth, Ronald E. *God's Word and Our Words.* Atlanta: John Knox, 1986.

Stott, John R. W. *Between Two Worlds.* Grand Rapids: Eerdmans, 1982.

Troeger, Thomas H. *Imagining a Sermon.* Nashville: Abingdon, 1990.

Van Seters, Art, ed. *Preaching as a Social Act.* Nashville: Abingdon, 1988.

Wardlaw, Don M., ed. *Learning Preaching.* Lincoln, Neb.: Academy of Homiletics, 1989.

Wilson, Paul Scott. *Imagination of the Heart.* Nashville: Abingdon, 1988.